P9-CMY-811

The Crockin' Girls Slow Cookin' Companion

Slow Cookin' Companion

Yummy Recipes from Family, Friends, and Our Crockin' Community

By Nicole Sparks & Jenna Marwitz

Thanks Y'all

This journey has been a whirlwind! I want to thank my husband, Stanton, for riding the ride with me and taking on some of "Mama's load" while I was crockin'! I am so blessed to have you—we make a pretty great team! To my mama and daddy for encouraging me to "go for it" my whole life and supporting me during this time! To the grandparents of my babies (Peppie & Pop and CiCi & Poppy), thank you for your unending supply of love for the kids—never hesitating to come play or have a slumber party—and for the yummy recipes you contributed to this book!

A huge thank-you to "Bambi," Kari, NiNi, and Aunt Jace for lovin' on Stella and Spencer just like they're your own! To my Grammy and Grandma Stone, I know y'all are looking down on this and couldn't be prouder; you were both terrific cooks and a great inspiration to me. Spencer and Stella, Mama loves you more than you know; thanks for being such great kids and constant blessings to my life! To everyone who helped us do the "impossible" and put together this cookbook in such a short period of time . . . whew, we did it! And to our crockin' community, thanks for the support, contributions, and a shared love of crockin'. Y'all are amazing!

~Jenna Marwitz

I am extremely blessed to experience such an amazing journey and want to extend my thanks to a few special people who have helped me along the way. First and foremost, I give a HUGE thanks to my biggest supporter and fan, the love of my life, and my best friend, Kristopher Sparks. I could not do this without you! Thank you to my parents for instilling the "go get 'em" attitude in my life and for loving me unconditionally.

A big thanks to my Aunt Holly for always loving me and loving my kids like crazy and for all those last-minute calls like, "Can you pick up my kids today?" Thanks to my Nanee and Pop for being there for me every second of my life—and always letting me lick the beaters! (Nanee, I just know you are in heaven smiling from ear to ear.) Thank you to both sides of my extended family for giving me the encouraging words and love to keep going. Thank you to my Gage and Gracie for providing me with all the hugs and kisses a mama could ask for. Thanks to my dear Savior for blessing Jenna and me with the ability to reach out and help provide an easier way for busy families to get a home-cooked meal on the table.

I am thankful every day that this journey is enabling me to give back to someone else. I am also so grateful to have my crockin' partner, Jenna Marwitz, and her precious family in my life. And to our supportive crockin' community, thank you for letting us crock with you!

~Nicole Sparks

Special Thanks

Our deepest gratitude goes to Mark Hulme at The Five Star Institute for recognizing the importance of getting families back around the table and helping us make our crockin' dreams a reality. To Brent Lockhart, who along the way has eagerly taken on many tasks in the production of this project. A special thanks to Alison Rich and Christi Steckel for taking our thoughts and ideas and putting them on paper for us to share with our crockin' community. Many thanks to the very talented art directors at Five Star who made this cook book look so yummy; Sean Walker, Jason Stone, Jonathon Won, Bruce Sons, Bee Loha-unchit, and Scott Walker. A final thanks to the wonderful Kimberly Dendy for organizing the Crock-A-Thon and Russell "Russ" Parr for helping prepare recipes, we couldn't have done it without you.

The Crockin' Girls Slow Cookin' Companion.

1909 Woodall Rodgers, Suite 300 Dallas, Texas 75201. Join the Crockin' Girls Club
and learn more at www.crockingirls.com

Creative Director: Sean Walker

Designed by Jason Stone, Jonathon Won, Bruce Lee Sons, Chanyanont Loha-unchit, Scott Walker

Photography by Stephen Dux and Jason Gamble

Photography Assistance by Brandon Jones

Food Styling by Sharon Sharp, Shannon Sharp, Jessica Maittre, Dean Smith

Recipe Testing Coordinated by Kimberly Dendy

Published by The Five Star Institute

Library of Congress Control Number 2012932943
ISBN 978-0-9849614-0-5
Printed in China

Crockin' Contents

Introduction

Hey, y'all, and welcome to our first-ever cookbook, *The Crockin' Girls' Slow Cookin' Companion*. To say that we're immensely excited and incredibly blessed would be the understatement of the century! Because while we now can add "cookbook authors" to our list of life's accomplishments, we're mamas, wives, sisters and daughters first and foremost. And we never, ever imagined that our lives would take such an amazing twist as this.

Inside these pages are 165 family-friendly recipes that we hope you'll enjoy preparing and eating as much as we do. While many come straight from our home kitchens to yours, a bunch were lovingly contributed by our sweet families, as well as precious members of our Crockin' Community.

From yummy appetizers and side dishes to tummy-tempting main meals and some of the most incredible desserts you've ever tasted, these recipes offer a special treat for every taste bud (and that includes the little buds, too!). The one thing they all have in common? Every single recipe is designed especially for your slow-cooker—the most amazing appliance ever made, by the way! Just plug it in, place in your ingredients, put on the lid and you're free to go on with your day. Then . . . presto! In just a few short hours, you've got a nutritious, delicious, stress-free meal ready to enjoy with your loved ones. It just doesn't get better than that.

As we like to say, "You can't go wrong when you have full bellies and full hearts!" We think you'll agree.

Happy Crockin', y'all!

Jenna and Nicole

Crock-a-doodle-doooooo, good morning to you! With four kiddos between us, mornings are eventful in our homes—to say the least! Whether we're hustling to get out the door or just want to spend the morning relaxing with our families, a crockin' breakfast really hits the spot. Kids love the Sunrise Pizza because they can help prepare the recipe. (And, besides, who doesn't love pizza for breakfast?) The ability to start most of these dishes the night before and wake up to the wonderful aroma of breakfast in the slow cooker is a major bonus in our homes. The Southwest Breakfast Casserole is always a crowd pleaser, and the Banana Nut Bread will surely have everyone waking up on the right side of the bed.

Good Morning, Sunshine

Breakfast

Nicole's Crockin' Breakfast

Kick-start your day with this fun and filling morning meal.

Breakfast

Ingredients

1 (32-ounce) package frozen diced hash browns

1 pound breakfast sausage, slightly browned

2 cups diced ham

2 cups fresh baby spinach

½ cup chopped fresh mushrooms

½ cup chopped onion

2 cups cheddar cheese

1 can diced tomatoes with green chiles

18 well-beaten eggs

Directions

Spray slow-cooker with non-stick cooking spray. Layer half the package of hash browns; half of browned sausage; half of ham; all of the spinach, mushrooms, and onion; and 1 cup of cheese. Once again, layer hash browns, sausage, and ham, and then pour diced tomatoes with green chiles over the top. Add beaten eggs and top with remaining cheese. Cook on LOW for 8 hours.

Banana Nut Bread

This recipe is made frequently at Nicole's house because her son, Gage, loves this dish.

Ingredients

3 bananas, mashed

1 ½ cups sugar

1 stick margarine, melted

2 eggs

1 teaspoon baking soda

1 teaspoon vanilla

2 cups flour

1 cup chopped nuts

You will need a 4 x 8-inch rectangle pan for this recipe.

Directions

Mix ingredients in a bowl in the following order: bananas, sugar, margarine, eggs, baking soda, vanilla, flour, and nuts. Spray loaf pan with non-stick cooking spray. Pour batter in pan and cover with foil. Place pan in slow-cooker. Pour water around the pan until it reaches about ¼ of the way up the side of the pan. Cook on HIGH for approximately 3 hours (or until toothpick comes out clean). Remove pan from slow-cooker and let cool. When cool, remove bread from pan. Slice and serve.

Breakfast

Southwest Breakfast Casserole

Ingredients

1 pound cooked breakfast sausage

1 small can green chiles

1 medium onion, diced

1 medium green pepper, diced

2 ½ cups grated cheese (whatever kind you prefer)

18 eggs, whisked, with salt and pepper added (if desired)

Directions

Layer first 5 ingredients (with cheese on the top of each layer), then top the entire breakfast casserole with the 18 eggs. Cook on LOW for about 8 hours.

Sweet Stella's Strudel

Sugar and spice and everything nice . . . that's what this recipe (named after Jenna's darling daughter) is made of.

Ingredients

flour (for dusting)

1 roll refrigerated thin-crust pizza dough

1 can cherry pie filling

1 (8-ounce) container whipped cream cheese

1 teaspoon vanilla

¼ cup sugar

1 egg, beaten

foil (to wrap up strudel)

sprinkles (optional)

Directions

Flour your work surface. Lay out dough and sprinkle with flour, then flip sides. In a medium bowl, mix the cherry pie filling, whipped cream cheese, vanilla, and sugar. In a small bowl, beat the egg. Spread cherry mixture over dough, covering about ⅔ of the dough. Begin rolling, starting at the end of the dough that has the mixture on it. Brush egg on the end that has no cherry mixture and close strudel. Brush egg along the outside edge and on the ends to seal. Top with sprinkles. Dust a piece of foil with flour and place the strudel on it. Roll tightly, twisting the ends of the foil like a candy wrapper. Place in the slow-cooker and cook on HIGH for 2 to 3 hours. Open foil, slice, and serve.

Sunrise Pizza

Waking up isn't a chore with this sunny surprise on the breakfast plate.

Ingredients

1 package refrigerated pizza dough

2 tablespoons butter, melted

4-6 eggs, scrambled

crumbled bacon

little smokies

⅓ cup diced onion

shredded cheese

Directions

Coat the slow-cooker with non-stick cooking spray. Roll out pizza dough and place in the bottom of the slow-cooker, pushing the dough up the sides of the slow-cooker to form the rim of the pizza. Baste crust with melted butter. Mix eggs, bacon, little smokies, onions, and cheese together and place mixture on top of dough. (Note from Nicole: When I scramble eggs or fry bacon, I always make extra for recipes like this.) Cover and cook on HIGH for 1 to 2 hours, or until pizza dough is done.

Gage and Gracie's Gooey Goodness

Nicole's kiddos love this finger-lickin' good recipe. They could eat a whole crock full!

Ingredients

- 1 stick butter, melted
- 1 cup dark Karo syrup
- ⅔ cup brown sugar
- 1 ½ to 2 cups pecans
- 1 to 2 packages of crescent rolls
- 1 tablespoon melted butter
- ½ to 1 cup sugar
- cinnamon, for sprinkling

Directions

Place the first 4 ingredients in the bottom of the slow-cooker. Unroll the crescent rolls until they make two individual rectangles. (They are normally in individual triangles if you separate them, but leave them together.) Baste with melted butter and sprinkle with as much sugar and cinnamon as your heart (or kids' hearts) desire. Roll up the rectangles, with the seam facing down. Start slicing the rolls to make individual cinnamon rolls. Place the individual rolls on the gooey pecan mixture. Keep adding rolls until the bottom of the slow-cooker and the gooey mixture are covered. Cover and cook on HIGH for 1 ½ to 2 hours, or until the rolls are not doughy. Dish onto a serving plate; all the yummy gooeyness will top the rolls.

Spencer's Special

The namesake for this kid-friendly recipe is Jenna's adorable son, who eats it right up because he likes having "hot dogs" with his breakfast!

Ingredients

1 bag shredded hash browns

1 package little smokies, cut in thirds

1 cup diced ham

1 small onion, chopped

1 small bell pepper, chopped

1 dozen eggs, well-beaten with salt and pepper

2 cups shredded cheese (your preference)

Directions

Combine all ingredients in the slow-cooker except for eggs and cheese. Pour eggs over the mixture and top with cheese. Cook on LOW for 8 hours.

Apple Cinnamon Steel-Cut Oatmeal

Ingredients

2 cups steel-cut oats

4 cups water

5 cups milk (may use skim)

1 large honey crisp apple cut into ½-inch pieces

1 teaspoon cinnamon

1 teaspoon vanilla

½ teaspoon salt

Directions

Combine all in the slow-cooker and cook on LOW overnight, 7 to 8 hours.

Submitted by Shirley Martin

Apple Butter

This fantastic recipe is precisely why we are so fond of our slow-cookers: They can revamp an age-old formula in 21st century style!

Ingredients

6 pounds peeled apples, thinly sliced

3 cups brown sugar

2 teaspoons ground cinnamon

¼ teaspoon ground cloves

Directions

Heap apples into the slow-cooker but leave enough room for the lid to fit snugly. Combine the brown sugar, cinnamon, and cloves; mix into the apples. Cover and cook on LOW for 2 to 3 hours, stirring occasionally. At the end of the cooking, mash any apple chunks with a potato masher or hand mixer, then cover and cook on HIGH for 1 hour. Pour into hot jars, adjust the lids, and boil in a hot-water bath for 10–15 minutes. Makes approximately 6 pints.

Submitted by Jeanie O'Bryan

Morning Casserole

Ingredients

1 (16-ounce) bag frozen hash brown potatoes

½ pound bacon, cooked, drained, and crumbled and/or ½ pound cooked diced ham

½ medium onion, diced

½ green bell pepper, diced

¾ cup shredded cheddar cheese

6 eggs, beaten

½ cup milk

½ teaspoon salt

½ teaspoon pepper

Directions

Spray the slow-cooker with non-stick cooking spray. Place a layer of frozen potatoes on the bottom of the slow-cooker, followed by a layer of bacon/ham (whatever meat you choose), then onions, green pepper, and cheese. Repeat layering process, ending with a layer of cheese. Beat together eggs, milk, and salt and pepper. Pour over mixture and cook on LOW for 8 hours.

Submitted by Lisa Bizaillion

Crockin' Oats

Wake up to a wonderful warm smell, and breakfast is ready!

Ingredients

1 cup steel-cut oats
5 cups water
¼ teaspoon salt
2 to 3 tablespoons butter
1 cup dried fruits and nuts
¼ cup brown sugar

Directions

Using a 2-quart slow-cooker, combine all ingredients and cook on LOW for 7 to 8 hours. Best when made the evening before.

Substitutions

(Choose from the following)

2 tablespoons brown sugar and some peanut butter

More water and no butter for a healthier version

Vanilla extract and some honey

Freshly chopped apples, pecans, a handful of raisins, and some cinnamon

Any fruit you like

Submitted by Michelle Noonan

Baked Fruit

A Huttenga family favorite, this is yum-a-licious as a dessert, side, over ice cream, or even on waffles.

Ingredients

1 can cherry pie filling

1 can applesauce (Carmen uses 1 ½ cups)

1 can pineapple tidbits, drained

1 large can peaches, drained

1 large can pears, drained

2 cans mandrin oranges, drained

½ cup brown sugar

3 tablespoons tapioca

1 teaspoon cinnamon

Directions

Place all ingredients in the slow-cooker; stir. Cook on LOW for 2 to 3 hours, or until hot and bubbly.

Submitted by *Carmen Huttenga*

Raceday Breakfast Casserole

Ingredients

1 (32-ounce) bag frozen potatoes

1 pound bacon, cooked and diced

2 pounds sausage, cooked

8 ounces cheddar cheese, shredded

1 dozen eggs, beaten

1 cup milk

1 teaspoon salt

1 teaspoon pepper

Directions

First, put a liner in your slow-cooker, which helps with clean up and no mess. Place a layer of frozen potatoes in the bottom of the slow-cooker, followed by a layer of bacon, sausage, and then cheese. Repeat layering until ingredients are gone, ending with a layer of cheese. Beat the eggs, milk, salt, and pepper together, and then pour over the mixture already in the slow-cooker. Cover and cook on LOW for 7 to 8 hours. Hint: if the top of the casserole looks a little greasy on the edges when finished cooking, take a piece of bread to soak it up.

Submitted by Heidi Bradford

Just a Taste

Come on over! Entertaining a crowd is something we both love to do, but we want to be out visiting with our guests, not stuck in the kitchen! With the slow-cooker, we can just throw together ingredients to make a tasty dip or bite-sized delights and join the fun. The best part is they stay warm throughout the party. Before you know it, everyone will be surrounding the slow-cooker and taking "just one more bite." Look for Nicole's favorite recipe from her Nanny McCue's kitchen, Sweet and Sour Meatballs, and one of Jenna's favorites from a past Crockin' Monday video, Cheesy Spinach Artichoke Dip. Game night, birthdays, or just hanging out is a good enough excuse for us to bring together family and friends for a crockin' good time.

Appetizers

Faith's Dip

Ingredients

½ block Velveeta cheese

1 package cream cheese

1 can cream of mushroom soup

1 can diced tomatoes with green chiles

1 pound sausage, crumbled and browned

Directions

Place all ingredients in the slow-cooker and heat on LOW until heated through. Serve with your choice of chips.

From Nicole's sister's kitchen

Sweet and Sour Meatballs

Nicole inherited this recipe when she married her hubby, Kris, and good thing because it's delicious. This family favorite will soon become your favorite, too.

Ingredients

4 pounds ground beef

2 eggs, beaten

1 onion, chopped

2 slices white sandwich bread, soaked in water and squeezed dry

salt and pepper, to taste

Sauce

1 (10-ounce) jar grape jelly

1 (12-ounce) bottle of chili sauce

juice of 1 lemon

Directions

Blend all but sauce ingredients and form into balls. Place the meatballs in the slow-cooker. Mix sauce ingredients together and pour over the meatballs. Cook on LOW for 6 to 8 hours.

From Nicole's Nanny McCue's kitchen

Cheesy Spinach Artichoke Dip

Serve in a bread bowl for a crowd-pleasing presentation.

Ingredients

1 can artichoke hearts, drained and chopped

1 pound frozen spinach, thawed and chopped

2 blocks cream cheese

2 ½ cups Monterey Jack cheese, cubed

2 ½ cups mozzarella cheese, shredded

3 teaspoons minced garlic

pepper, to taste

Directions

Place all ingredients in the slow-cooker and cook on HIGH for 1 to 2 hours, or until cheese is melted. Stir occasionally. Serve with crackers, chips, or bread.

Bacon-Wrapped Smokies

Quick, easy, and great for gatherings. What's not to love about this all-time favorite finger food?!

Ingredients

1 package uncooked bacon

1 to 2 packages little smokies (we like the turkey variety)

2 cups brown sugar

toothpicks

Directions

Cut bacon into thirds. Take the individual bacon pieces and wrap 1 piece around 1 little smokie; secure with a toothpick until all smokies have been wrapped. Place brown sugar on the bottom of the slow-cooker and add a layer of smokies, repeating layers of brown sugar and smokies until all gone. Cook on HIGH for 2 to 3 hours, or until bacon is fully cooked, stirring occasionally.

Groundhog Cheese Dip

Just like the famous movie of the same name, when you sample this delicious dip, you'll want to relive the day over and over again.

Ingredients

1 pound ground beef

1 pound sausage

1 pound Velveeta cheese

1 pound Velveeta Mexican cheese

1 can diced tomatoes with green chiles

½ jar salsa

1 can cream of mushroom soup

Directions

Brown ground beef and sausage; drain and place in the slow-cooker. Cube cheese and place in the slow-cooker. Mix together the remaining ingredients and place in the slow-cooker. Cook on LOW for 4 hours or until cheese is melted. Stir frequently and serve with chips.

Submitted by Melisa Quates

Barbecue Chicken Sliders

Slide into snack time with this tasty treat for kids and adults!

Ingredients

3 large boneless, skinless chicken breasts

1 bottle of your favorite barbecue sauce

1 can cream of chicken soup

1 to 2 packages prepared dinner rolls

Garnish with your choice of the following: lettuce, tomatoes, pickles, onion

Directions

Place chicken breasts in the slow-cooker. Pour soup and barbecue sauce over the chicken. Cook on LOW for 6 to 8 hours; shred chicken when fully cooked. Slice dinner rolls and stuff with barbecue chicken. Add desired garnish.

Crab Dip

Ingredients

1 (8-ounce) package cream cheese, softened

½ cup finely chopped sweet onion

¼ cup Parmesan cheese

¼ cup mayonnaise

2 garlic cloves, minced

2 teaspoons sugar

1 (6-ounce) can crabmeat, drained, flaked, and cartilage removed

Assorted crackers for dipping

Directions

In a 1-to 2-quart slow-cooker, combine the first six ingredients; stir in crab. Cover and cook on LOW for 2 to 3 hours, or until heated through.

Submitted by Lannie Steinbacher

Championship Bean Dip

This is a crunch-tastic solution for serving a houseful of folks gathered to watch the big game.

Ingredients

1 (16-ounce) can refried beans

1 cup picante sauce

1 cup shredded Monterey Jack cheese

1 cup shredded cheddar cheese

¾ cup sour cream

1 (3-ounce) package cream cheese, softened

1 tablespoon chili powder

¼ teaspoon ground cumin

Directions

In a bowl, combine all the ingredients and transfer to the slow-cooker. Cover and cook on LOW for 2 hours, or until heated through, stirring once or twice. Serve with tortilla chips and salsa.

Submitted by Lisa Short

Not Your Mama's Nachos

Ingredients

1 pound hamburger meat

½ can light beer (can be replaced with chicken broth)

1 small jar salsa, divided

1 packet taco seasoning

1 can corn, drained

1 can black beans, drained

tortilla chips, shredded cheese, sour cream, jalapeño slices

Directions

Put hamburger meat in the slow-cooker. Mix together beer, ½ bottle of salsa, and taco seasoning. Pour over meat. Top with corn, beans, and remaining salsa. Cook on LOW for 4 to 6 hours. Arrange nacho chips on plate; use slotted spoon to serve. Top with cheese, sour cream, and jalapeño slices.

Submitted by Dana Hallman

Appetizers

Cheesy Taco Dip

Ingredients

1 pound hamburger meat

1 pound sausage

1 onion, chopped

1 (32-ounce) jar salsa

2 small blocks Velveeta Mexican cheese

Directions

Brown hamburger meat and sausage until finely crumbled. Place all ingredients in the slow-cooker and cook on HIGH until cheese is melted. Serve with tortilla chips or corn chips. Keep on LOW while serving, stirring occasionally.

Submitted by *Amy Timm*

Spicy Crab Dip

This zippy dip gets some extra punch from green onions and hot sauce.

Ingredients

2 (6-ounce) cans crabmeat

1 (8-ounce) package cream cheese, softened

1 bunch green onions, chopped

1 (16-ounce) container sour cream

2 cups sharp cheddar cheese (save ½ cup for topping)

2 tablespoons hot sauce

2 tablespoons Morton Nature's Seasons

½ teaspoon garlic powder

Directions

Combine all ingredients in the slow-cooker and cook on LOW for 1 to 2 hours. Add remaining cheese during the last hour. Cook until cheese is melted. Serve with crackers or veggies.

Submitted by *Andra Hagensen*

Chicken Dip

Extra chicken in the fridge? This is a handy (and yummy) way to use it up.

Ingredients

- 5 cooked chicken breasts, shredded
- 2 (16-ounce) jars of salsa
- 1 can corn, drained
- 1 can black beans, drained
- 2 small cans green chiles, diced
- 1 package taco seasoning

Directions

Combine all the ingredients in the slow-cooker. Cook on LOW for 5 hours or on HIGH for 3 hours.

Optional items to serve with

- black olives
- shredded cheese
- sour cream
- shredded lettuce
- tortilla chips

Submitted by Sue Moen

Eagle Dip

A snap to throw together for last-minute menus, this stellar dip soars above the same-old, same-old.

Ingredients

1 pound ground beef, browned and drained

1 package taco seasoning

1 can refried beans

8 ounces shredded cheddar cheese

1 cup cooked rice

1 jar salsa

Directions

Mix together all the ingredients in the slow-cooker. Cook on LOW for 2 to 3 hours, or until dip is hot and cheese is melted. Serve with tortilla chips.

Submitted by Michelle Lahr

Buffalo Chicken Dip

Expect a herd of hungry eaters to dive into your slow-cooker right after you lift off the lid.

Ingredients

1 (8-ounce) package cream cheese, softened

¾ cup blue cheese dressing

½ cup blue cheese crumbles

½ cup buffalo wing sauce

1 pound boneless, skinless chicken breasts, cooked and shredded

½ cup chopped celery

Directions

In a 3-quart slow-cooker, mix cream cheese, blue cheese dressing, blue cheese crumbles, and wing sauce. Stir in chicken and cover. Heat on LOW for 1 hour, or until cheese is melted and dip is heated through. Stir in celery. Serve with chips of your choice or celery.

Submitted by Michelle Hulke

Finger Lickin' Bites

Add this three-ingredient dish to your lineup for a "grape escape" from the ho-hum.

Ingredients

1 package meatballs or 2 packages little smokies

2 (12-ounce) jars chili sauce

1 (16-ounce) jar grape jelly

Directions

Mix together the chili sauce and grape jelly; pour over meatballs or smokies and cook on HIGH for 2 hours, or until meat is heated through. Reduce heat to LOW to ensure that all grape jelly has melted completely.

Submitted by Kimberly Legg

Tara's Yummy Cheese Dip

Our Crockin' pal Tara took an all-time fave and upped the ante with a surprise ingredient . . . whipped cream!

Ingredients

1 block Velveeta cheese, cubed (whatever flavor you prefer)

1 to 2 cans diced tomatoes with green chiles

2 cans chili without beans

1 large container whipped cream

Directions

Put cheese, tomatoes, and chili in the slow-cooker; cook on LOW for 1 hour, stirring frequently. When cheese is almost melted, add the whipped cream. Cook on LOW for an additional 30 minutes, then turn to WARM until completely hot. Serve with chips, crackers, or pieces of bread for fondue.

Submitted by Tara McLellan

Idaho Dip

Representing the Gem State, this easy-does-it dip gets two huge thumbs up whenever Kim cooks it.

Ingredients

1 package sausage, spicy or mild

2 packages cream cheese

1 can diced tomatoes with green chilies, mild or hot

Directions

Cook sausage in skillet until done. Place in the slow-cooker, along with cream cheese and diced tomatoes with green chiles. Cook on LOW for 2 hours, or until heated through. Serve with your favorite chips or crackers.

Submitted by *Kim Orge*

Spinach Dip

Ingredients

1 (9-ounce) package frozen creamed spinach (heated in microwave, according to package directions)

3 ounces regular cream cheese

½ cup grated Parmesan (plus an additional 1 tablespoon on top)

¼ cup light mayonnaise

2 tablespoons finely chopped green onions

¾ cup Monterey Jack cheese, shredded

Directions

Combine the hot spinach, cream cheese, ½ cup Parmesan cheese, mayonnaise, and green onions in the slow-cooker; stir well. Sprinkle Monterey Jack cheese and the remaining 1 tablespoon Parmesan cheese on top. Cook on LOW for about 2 hours, or until hot and cheese is melted. Serve with Hawaiian bread, tortilla chips, or crackers.

Submitted by Jean Hartman

ZEPHYR
BULLDOGS

Bowls of Goodness

When you want simple and easy, you can't go wrong with a bowl of your favorite soup, stew, or chili. Most of the ingredients are usually on hand, so they're easy to fix and make enough to feed a small army. Jenna's Chicken Tortilla Soup is hearty with loads of flavor and a dish we always seem to crave. If you're crockin' for a smaller crowd, just freeze half and you instantly have a ready-to-go meal saved for a rainy day. Best of all, after you've taken more than your share of "tastes" to make sure it's ready, just serve it in a single dish and you're done. Less dishes to clean and more time to think about the next recipe you'll make.

Soups, Stews, & Chili

Jenna's Chicken Tortilla Soup

Jenna and her crew love coming home to the aroma of this crockin' classic after a long day out and about.

Ingredients

2 to 3 cups raw chicken, cut into 1-inch pieces

1 can diced tomatoes with green chilies

1 (8-ounce) can tomato sauce

2 (14.5-ounce) cans chicken broth

1 can cheddar cheese soup

2 cups carrots (Jenna uses the "carrot chips" that are cut like pickles and cuts them in half)

½ bag frozen corn

1 large onion, chopped

2 cloves garlic, minced

¼ teaspoon ground cumin

½ tablespoon chili powder

cilantro (Jenna just chops up a handful)

Salt and pepper, to taste

Garnishes
2 avocados cut into small bites
shredded cheese
tortilla chips

Directions

Combine all ingredients in the slow-cooker, except for the garnishes. Cook on HIGH for about 5 to 6 hours or on LOW for about 8 hours. Ladle into bowls and top each serving with avocado, cheese, and tortilla chips.

Nicole's Corn Chowder

Nicole's kiddos (and her hubby, too!) are big fans of this corny creation. Try some Crockin' Cornbread on the side for a satisfying supper.

Ingredients

6 to 8 potatoes, peeled and cubed

1 can creamed corn

1 can whole kernel corn, drained

2 cups chicken broth

8 ounces diced ham

1 cup diced onions

salt and pepper, to taste

¼ cup butter

1 to 2 cups half-and-half (to the consistency of your liking)

Directions

Place potatoes, both cans of corn, chicken broth, ham, and onions into the slow-cooker. Cook on LOW for 7 to 8 hours. Mash the mixture to your desired consistency and then add the butter and half-and-half. Cook on HIGH for an additional 30 minutes.

Loaded Baked Potato Soup

Ingredients

- 6 large potatoes, peeled and cubed
- 1 large onion, diced
- 1 quart chicken broth
- 3 garlic cloves, minced
- ¼ cup butter
- salt and pepper, to taste
- 1 cup cream or 1 cup half-and-half
- 1 cup shredded sharp cheddar cheese
- Toppings: chives, sour cream, bacon, cheese

Directions

Combine all ingredients except cream or half-and-half and cheddar cheese in slow-cooker. Cook on HIGH for 4 hours or on LOW for 8 hours (potatoes should be tender). Mash potatoes until coarsely chopped and soup is slightly thickened. Stir in cream or half-and-half and cheese. Garnish with toppings.

Thankful Fiesta Soup

Transform your leftover Thanksgiving bird into a bountiful bowl of soup. (Or grab some turkey from your grocer's freezer during any month of the year. It's that good!)

Ingredients

3 to 4 cups turkey, chopped

20 ounces chicken broth

1 can black beans, drained

1 can whole kernel corn, drained

2 (10-ounce) cans diced tomatoes with green chilies

1 can tomato paste

1 can cream of mushroom soup or cream of chicken soup

4 ounces queso blanco Velveeta cheese

Pepper, ground cumin, and garlic powder, to taste

Directions

Mix together all ingredients in the slow-cooker. Cook on HIGH for 3 hours, or until ingredients are heated through.

Taco Stew

We give this one a Texas-size thumbs up!

Ingredients

1 pound ground beef

1 (15-ounce) can pinto beans, drained

1 (15-ounce) can Ranch Style beans, drained

1 (10-ounce) can diced tomatoes with green chilies

1 (14.5-ounce) can diced tomatoes

1 can corn, drained

1 packet taco seasoning

1 packet ranch dressing seasoning mix

salt and pepper, to taste

Directions

Combine all ingredients in the slow-cooker. Cook on HIGH for 4 hours or on LOW for approximately 6 hours.

Chicken and Dumplings

You can make your own dumplings from scratch. But if you're pressed for time (we can relate), use a can of biscuits!

Ingredients

4 boneless, skinless chicken breasts

2 tablespoons butter

1 (10.75-ounce) can cream of chicken soup

1 (10.75-ounce) can cream of celery soup

3 ½ cups chicken broth

1 onion, finely diced

1 cup celery, diced

1 cup carrots, sliced

2 chicken bouillon cubes

1 (10-ounce) can refrigerated biscuits

salt and pepper, to taste

Directions

Excluding the biscuits, put all ingredients in the slow-cooker. Cover and cook on LOW for 8 hours. About an hour before serving, remove chicken and pull into pieces; return to the soup mixture. Place the torn biscuit dough into the slow-cooker and cook until dough is no longer raw in the center.

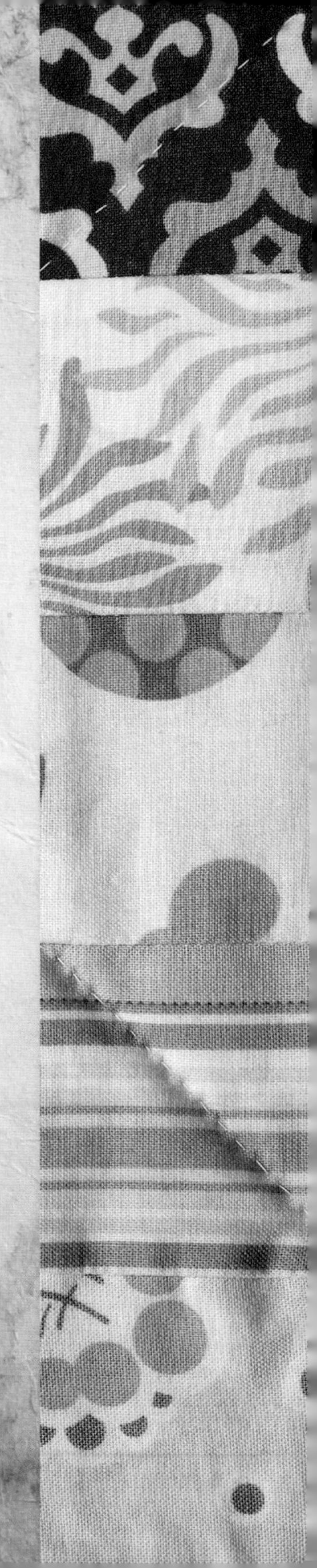

Campfire Stew

This robust bowl of yumminess will have you feeling like a seasoned camper—minus the tent and sleeping bags!

Ingredients

- 1 to 2 pounds ground beef, browned and drained
- 1 onion, chopped
- 3 to 4 potatoes, peeled and chopped
- 1 large package frozen mixed vegetables
- 1 small package frozen sliced okra
- 1 can whole kernel corn
- 1 to 2 cans diced tomatoes
- 1 small can tomato sauce
- salt and pepper, to taste

Directions

Place all ingredients in the slow-cooker. Cover with water to approximately 1 inch above ingredients. Cook on HIGH for 6 to 8 hours.

From Nicole's mom's kitchen

Jalapeño Soup

If you want to save time when you cook this again, you can prep several pounds of chicken, then place in freezer bags and use whenever the fancy strikes!

Ingredients

1 chopped onion

1 chicken breast

4 cups chicken broth

2 cans cream of celery soup

1 teaspoon garlic salt

2 pounds cubed cheddar cheese or 4 cups shredded cheddar cheese (Velveeta or a natural shredded cheese works best)

1 cup diced jalapeño peppers, or other green chiles like poblano, for less zing

1 teaspoon white pepper (optional)

Directions

Sauté onion and cook with chicken breast. Cut chicken into cubes. Spray slow-cooker with nonstick cooking spray; add all ingredients to slow-cooker except cheese and jalapeños. Cook on HIGH for 1 to 2 hours or on LOW for 4 to 6 hours, or until mixture is thickened. Slowly and carefully stir cheese into soup, mixing constantly for a smooth consistency. Cook on LOW for another 30 to 60 minutes. Stir mixture and add jalapeños, or other peppers, if desired. Cook on LOW for an additional 15 minutes. May add flour or milk to change consistency to your preference. Serve with tortilla chips, a dollop of sour cream, and optional green onions.

Tater Soup

Ingredients

1 (30-ounce) bag frozen hash brown potatoes

2 (14-ounce) cans chicken broth

1 can cream of potato soup

½ cup carrots, chopped

½ teaspoon garlic, minced

⅓ teaspoon pepper

1 (8-ounce) package cream cheese, softened

Garnishes: crumbled bacon, cheddar cheese, minced green onion

Directions

In a 6-quart slow-cooker, combine potatoes, broth, soup, carrots, garlic, and pepper. Cover and cook on LOW for 5 hours. Stir in cream cheese and cook another 30 minutes, stirring occasionally until combined. Garnish as desired.

Submitted by Samantha Parisi

Buffalo Chicken Soup

This substantial soup is the ideal solution for a chilly day. (Of course, it tastes pretty great when the weather's warm, too!)

Ingredients

1 tablespoon oil
1 large onion, chopped
3 stalks celery, diced
2 to 3 cups cooked chicken, diced
¼ cup butter
¼ cup flour
1 cup chicken broth
2 cups milk
1 teaspoon garlic salt
1 cup bottled buffalo wing sauce (mild or hot)
4 ounces shredded cheddar cheese

Directions

Heat oil in large skillet over medium heat. Add onion and celery and sauté for about 5 minutes. Scrape veggies into the slow-cooker. Add cooked chicken to the slow-cooker. Melt butter in skillet over medium heat just until foamy. Whisk in the flour to make a roux, stirring well to incorporate all the flour. Cook 1 to 2 minutes, or until the roux is slightly golden. Scrape into the slow-cooker. Stir in broth and milk. Add garlic salt and wing sauce. Stir well. Cover and cook on LOW for 6 to 8 hours or on HIGH for 3 to 4 hours. Stir in cheese about 20 minutes before serving.

Submitted by Anne Block

Broccoli Cheese Soup

Our cookbook wouldn't be complete without this best-loved soup. And slow-cookin' makes it even better!

Ingredients

3 cans cream of potato soup

2 cans chicken broth

1 can cream of celery soup

1 pound Velveeta cheese, cubed

8 ounces sour cream

1 box frozen chopped broccoli

handful of grated or chopped carrots

Directions

Add all ingredients to the slow-cooker. Cook on LOW for 3 to 4 hours, stirring every 30 minutes.

Submitted By Kyra Newberry

Chicken and Wild Rice Soup

It's so convenient to make a big batch of this when you're hankering for goodness in a bowl.

Ingredients

1 large onion, chopped
4 carrots, chopped
2 celery ribs, chopped
¼ cup butter
¼ teaspoon salt
¼ teaspoon pepper
½ cup flour
8 cups chicken broth
3 cups wild rice (Michelle uses two whole-grain rice microwavable pouches and cooks as directed before adding to slow-cooker)
2 cups cubed chicken breast
1 cup fat-free evaporated milk

Directions

In a large saucepan, sauté onion, carrots, and celery in butter until tender; add salt and pepper while cooking. Stir in flour until blended. Add mixture to the slow-cooker, then add broth, rice, chicken, and milk. Cook on HIGH for 3 to 4 hours or on LOW for 5 to 6 hours.

Submitted by Michelle Devine

Gluten-Free Chili

We can't begin to tell you how many requests we get for gluten-free recipes. What's great about this one is everyone (dietary-restricted or not) will gobble it up.

Ingredients

- 2 pounds ground beef
- 2 cans flavored diced tomatoes, (1 jalapeño, 1 Italian)
- 2 cans light kidney beans, drained and rinsed
- 1 (8-ounce) can tomato sauce
- 1 jar chili sauce
- 2 stalks celery, chopped
- 1 medium purple onion, chopped
- 4 cloves garlic, minced
- 1 bell pepper, chopped
- 4 tablespoons Worcestershire sauce
- 2 teaspoons salt
- 2 tablespoons paprika
- 4 teaspoons sugar
- 4 teaspoons dried basil
- 2 teaspoons dried oregano
- 1 teaspoon cumin
- 1 teaspoon celery salt
- dash of cayenne pepper

Directions

Brown the ground beef; drain and pour into the slow-cooker. Add the remaining ingredients and cook on LOW for about 7 to 8 hours. Serve with Crockin' Cornbread or corn tortillas. Sprinkle grated cheese on top of each bowl, if desired.

Submitted by Libby Sosinski

Mexican Bean Soup

Lean beef and a bounty of beans pack a good-for-you punch while the spices round out the recipe.

Ingredients

- 1 ½ pounds lean ground chuck, browned and drained
- 1 can black beans, drained
- 1 can dark red kidney beans, drained
- 2 cans Mexicorn, drained
- 1 can diced tomatoes with onion and green peppers, undrained
- 1 (12-ounce) jar chunky salsa
- Chicken broth (add until you achieve the desired soupiness)
- 1 teaspoon onion salt
- 1 teaspoon garlic powder
- salt and pepper, to taste
- Garnish with mexican blend shredded cheese and sour cream

Directions

Mix together all ingredients in the slow-cooker and let simmer on LOW for 3 to 4 hours. Serve with a little Mexican-blend shredded cheese and a dollop of sour cream.

Submitted by Beth Tovich

Gram's Soup

We love our sweet grandmas, so when we saw this meal-in-one recipe, we were so excited. And when we tasted it . . . wow!

Ingredients

1 to 1 ½ pounds ground chuck, browned and drained

½ to 1 cup chopped onions

½ package beef sausage, sliced very thin

1 can whole kernel corn, undrained

1 can pinto beans, undrained

1 can diced tomatoes with green chilies, undrained

Directions

Brown ground chuck with onions; place in the slow-cooker. Add the remaining ingredients and cook on LOW for 3 to 4 hours to blend the flavors and heat through. If it seems a bit thick, just add a little water. Serve with Crockin' Cornbread.

Submitted by Ella Ruth Morgan

K.O. Crockin' Chili

Texans love chili, and when we tasted Kelly's version, we were bowled over by its unique flavor.

Ingredients

1 pound ground turkey, browned
2 green peppers, chopped
1 large yellow onion, chopped
2 cans diced tomatoes
2 cans kidney beans
1 can chicken broth
1 (15-ounce) can tomato sauce
1 tablespoon garlic, minced
1 teaspoon chili powder
1 teaspoon pepper
1 tablespoon basil
Toppings
shredded cheese
sour cream
crackers

Directions

Combine all ingredients in the slow-cooker. Cook on HIGH for 3 to 4 hours or on LOW for 6 to 8 hours. Serve with toppings.

Submitted by Kelly Oliver

Hearty Hamburger Stew

The alternate name for this incredibly effortless recipe is "Whatever Is in the Fridge Stew." After you cook it, you'll understand why!

Ingredients

1 pound lean hamburger meat, browned

1 carton (or about 3 cans) beef or vegetable broth (can also use water and beef bouillon or vegetable paste)

1 can stewed tomatoes

4 to 5 garlic cloves, peeled and diced

1 cup diced carrots

1 cup diced onion

1 cup diced celery

1 cup shredded green cabbage

1 to 2 large baking potatoes, cubed

½ cup each frozen green beans, lima beans, peas

1 tablespoon Italian seasoning (dried oregano, basil, thyme, etc.)

salt and pepper, to taste

Directions

Put all ingredients into a large slow-cooker. Cook on LOW all day, or until you're ready to eat.

Submitted by Corey L. Dousharm

East Brunswick Stew

This traditional Southern stew gets a modern-day makeover, thanks to Ginny's super-simple technique.

Ingredients

- 1 large onion, chopped
- 1 pound ground beef, browned and drained
- 2 (15-ounce) cans creamed corn
- 2 (15-ounce) cans diced new potatoes
- 2 (15-ounce) cans petite diced tomatoes
- 2 (13-ounce) cans of chicken
- 1 (18-ounce) container shredded pork
- ¼ cup regular barbecue sauce
- 1 (24-ounce) bottle ketchup
- ¼ cup Worcestershire sauce
- 1 tablespoon apple cider vinegar
- 1 teaspoon salt
- ½ teaspoon pepper
- 1 (15-ounce) can lima beans (optional)

Directions

Place all ingredients in a 6-quart slow-cooker. Cook on LOW for 4 to 6 hours or on HIGH for 2 to 3 hours.

Submitted by Ginny Jones

Vegetable Stew

This nutrient-packed stew is a great way to sneak in a daily dose of veggies. (Your kids will never know!)

Ingredients

2 pounds cut stew meat

1 (16-ounce) can vegetable juice

1 onion, chopped

6 medium potatoes, cubed

3 carrots, cubed

1 can green beans

½ teaspoon garlic

Directions

Brown meat, then add it and the rest of the ingredients to the slow-cooker. Cook on LOW for 6 to 8 hours.

Submitted by *Randi Spoor*

Frito Pie

Crunchy, salty chips smothered in all sorts of appetizing additions . . . there's just no way to go wrong with this family-friendly favorite.

Ingredients

1 pound ground beef or turkey

½ sweet onion, chopped

1 can stewed tomatoes

2 cans pork and beans

1 package mild chili seasoning

Fritos

Toppings
colby Jack
shredded cheese
sour cream
black olives

Submitted by Brandie Richards

Directions

Brown the ground beef or turkey with the onion. Place meat and onion mixture into the slow cooker. Add the tomatoes, pork and beans, and the chili seasoning. Cook on LOW for 4 to 6 hours. After finished cooking, place the Fritos in the bottom of the bowl, cover with chili, and add toppings.

New Year's White Chicken Chili

Whether you're ringing in the year or (finally) resolving to spend more hours with your loved ones and less hours in the kitchen, this is the go-to bowl for you!

Ingredients

1 pound boneless, skinless chicken breasts

1 packet white chicken chili seasoning mix

1 medium onion, chopped

1 ½ teaspoons garlic powder

1 can low-sodium chicken broth

½ teaspoon salt

1 teaspoon cumin

1 teaspoon oregano

1 can sweet white corn, drained and rinsed

1 can black-eyed peas, drained and rinsed

1 cup sour cream

½ cup half-and-half

Garnishes
shredded Monterrey jack cheese
sour cream
lime wedges

Directions

Place chicken breasts in the slow-cooker. Sprinkle entire contents of seasoning packet on both sides of chicken breasts. Add chopped onion, garlic powder, chicken broth, salt, cumin, and oregano. Cook on LOW for 3 to 4 hours, then remove cooked chicken and shred. Return chicken to slow cooker. Add corn and black-eyed peas and stir well. Forty-five minutes before serving, stir in sour cream and half-and-half. Serve with garnishes and Crockin' Cornbread, if desired.

Submitted by Mary Beth Kloiber

Side by Side

What are the perfect complements and necessities at our dinner tables? Our other halves! Through it all, our loving husbands have been by our sides making this journey so fulfilling. They love our cookin' and love when their plates (and tummies!) are full. Creating a well-balanced meal for their hard-working appetites means having sides to go along with the main dish. Crockin' Cornbread is a good pairing everyone loves (Jenna likes hers with jelly), and the Green Bean Casserole will probably be the first thing they eat off their plates. If you're looking for mac and cheese recipes for the little mouths at the table, look no further—we have just what you need to make everyone happy.

Sides

Green Bean Casserole

This classic dish is a snap in the slow-cooker.

Ingredients

1 (28-ounce) package frozen cut green beans

1 onion, diced

2 cloves garlic, minced

1 red bell pepper, diced

1 (16-ounce) container alfredo cheesy sauce

1 (6-ounce) package french-fried onions

salt and pepper, to taste

Directions

Combine green beans, onion, garlic, bell pepper, alfredo sauce, ½ the package of french-fried onions, and salt and pepper in the slow-cooker; mix well. Cook on HIGH for 3 to 4 hours. Remove lid and sprinkle with the remaining french-fried onions. Continue to cook for another hour or serve immediately.

Crockin' Cornbread

This adaptable bread pairs beautifully with just about any of our crockin' meals.

Ingredients

1 small box cornbread mix

1 egg (as directed on box)

⅓ cup milk (as directed on box)

¼ cup sour cream

1 to 2 tablespoons sugar

Directions

Spray the slow-cooker with non-stick cooking spray, then preheat on HIGH for about 30 minutes. While the cooker is preheating, mix together the remaining ingredients until smooth. Pour the batter in the preheated slow-cooker; cover and cook on HIGH for about 1½–2 hours. When done, place a plate on top of the slow-cooker, then invert the slow-cooker to release the cornbread. Slice and serve.

Navy Beans

A perfect side to go with her mama's home cookin', these luscious legumes are high in protein—and flavor, too!

Ingredients

1 pound dry navy beans

2 tablespoons bacon grease

salt and pepper, to taste

2 tablespoons sugar (optional)

Directions

Place all of the ingredients in the slow-cooker and cover with water (about 3 inches above beans). Cook on HIGH for approximately 4 hours or on LOW for 8 hours.

From Jenna's mom's kitchen

Cheddar Mac

You'll ditch the boxed version for good the minute this hits your mouth.

Ingredients

1 (16-ounce) package macaroni

2 cups half-and-half

1 can cheese soup

½ cup butter, melted

4 cups shredded cheddar cheese

Directions

Cook pasta according to package directions and drain. Combine pasta with remaining ingredients and place in the slow-cooker. Cover and cook on LOW for 2 to 2½ hours.

Submitted by Becky Seibert

Baked Potatoes

When we're hungering for spuds, we always trade the oven for the slow-cooker.

Ingredients

4 to 6 medium to large russet potatoes

olive oil

kosher salt

foil

Directions

Poke holes in potatoes with a knife or fork. Rub with olive oil and then coat with kosher salt. Wrap in foil and place in the slow-cooker. Cover and cook on HIGH for about 4 to 5 hours (the potatoes will be tender). Serve with your choice of toppings.

Garlic Smashed Potatoes

Ingredients

3 pounds small red potatoes

5 garlic cloves, minced

1 onion, diced

Salt and pepper, to taste

2 tablespoons olive oil

⅔ cup water

1 cup cream cheese with onions and chives

2 tablespoons butter

½ cup milk or heavy whipping cream

Directions

Dice potatoes and place in the slow-cooker. Add garlic, onion, salt and pepper, olive oil, and water. Mix to coat. Cover and cook on HIGH for 3 to 4 hours, or until potatoes are tender. Remove lid and mash potatoes to desired consistency. Stir in cream cheese, butter, and milk or cream. Serve immediately or switch to LOW until ready to eat.

Cowboy Beans

Transform your table into a home on the range with this old-timey, Western-styled grub.

Ingredients

- ½ cup ketchup
- ½ cup brown sugar
- ½ cup white sugar
- 1 tablespoon dry mustard (can substitute with table mustard)
- 2 tablespoons vinegar
- ¼ teaspoon salt
- 1 pound hamburger meat, browned and drained
- ½ pound bacon, cooked, drained, and crumbled
- 1 medium onion, chopped
- 1 can lima beans, drained
- 1 can pork and beans, drained
- 1 can kidney beans, drained
- 1 can butter beans, drained

Directions

Mix ketchup, sugars, mustard, vinegar, and salt in a large mixing bowl. Add in (already cooked) meat, onions and beans and place in slow-cooker. Cover and cook on LOW for 3 to 4 hours or on HIGH for 1 to 2 hours.

Submitted by Nancy Koester

Mac 'n Corn

Your kids will flock to the kitchen when you spoon a serving of this side onto their plates!

Ingredients

1 can creamed corn

1 can regular corn, undrained

1 cup macaroni, uncooked

1 cup Velveeta cheese, cubed

1 stick butter

Directions

Add all ingredients to the slow-cooker. Cook on LOW for 4 hours, stirring occasionally.

Submitted by Tina Mosbey

Party Potatoes

Get ready for raves. These stellar spuds will be the life of your fiesta!

Ingredients

6 to 8 large potatoes

¼ to ½ cup butter

1 (8-ounce) package shredded cheddar cheese

1 bunch of green onions, chopped

1 (4-ounce) package real bacon pieces

salt and pepper, to taste

Directions

Wash and dry potatoes, wrap in foil, cut a slit in each one, and place in the slow-cooker. Cook on LOW for 8 hours or on HIGH for 4 hours. Remove potatoes from the cooker and unwrap. Remove potato skin and cut potatoes into bite-size pieces. Place liner in the slow-cooker and add back potatoes. Add the remaining ingredients and stir gently. Cook on LOW for an additional 20 to 30 minutes, or until cheese is melted through.

Submitted by *Melissa Casey*

Twice-Cooked Potatoes

Sure, they are doubly delicious, but still just as easy as the usual slow-cooker side.

Ingredients

6 large potatoes

1 pint sour cream

1 can cream of mushroom soup

1 cup grated cheddar cheese

½ cup green onions, chopped

salt and pepper, to taste

¼ cup melted butter

Directions

Peel and boil potatoes until cooked but still firm. Cool. Chop into large bowl; fold in all other ingredients except for butter. Spray slow-cooker with nonstick cooking spray, then add potato mixture. Pour melted butter over mixture. Cook on LOW for 3 to 4 hours.

Submitted by Lori Brooks Lear

Ham and Beans

Ingredients

1-pound package dry navy beans or dry great Northern beans

1 small ham hock, ham shank, or ham pieces

salt and pepper, to taste

Directions

Place the dry beans in a large saucepan or pot and completely cover with water; cover and leave to soak overnight. In the morning, rinse the beans and place in a 5-to 6-quart slow-cooker. Cover the beans with fresh water, then add the ham hock, shank, or pieces (as much as desired). Salt and pepper, to taste. Cook on LOW for 6 to 8 hours.

Submitted by Nikki Booth

Cheesy, Creamy Corn

There's greatness galore in this spoonable side.

Ingredients

2 (32-ounce) packages frozen corn

2 (8-ounce) packages cream cheese, cubed

¼ cup butter or margarine, cubed

4 tablespoons water

4 tablespoons milk

2 tablespoons sugar

9 slices American processed cheese, cut in pieces

Directions

Combine all the ingredients in the slow-cooker; mix well. Cover and cook on LOW for 4 hours, or until heated through and the cheese is melted. Stir well before serving.

Submitted by Laura Eniss

Cheesy Potatoes

Seriously, y'all, the cheesiness here is out of this world.

Ingredients

2-pound package frozen hash brown potatoes (partially thawed)

2 (10-ounce) cans cheddar cheese soup

1 (13-ounce) can evaporated milk

1 can french-fried onion rings

salt and pepper, to taste

Directions

Combine potatoes, soup, milk, and ½ of the onion rings. Pour into a 5-quart greased slow-cooker. Salt and pepper, to taste. Cover and cook on LOW for 8 to 9 hours or on HIGH for 3 to 4 hours, stirring occasionally. Sprinkle remaining onion rings on top before end of cooking or before serving.

Submitted by *LaRay Mason*

Good Beans

Ingredients

2 cups dried red beans (washed, picked over, and soaked in cold water overnight)

1 pound smoked sausage, thinly sliced, 1 pound browned beef, or 1 pound finely chopped smoked bacon

1 medium onion, finely chopped

4 cups broth (beef or chicken)

1 can diced tomatoes

garlic salt and pepper, to taste

1 poblano pepper, chopped, or 1 small jalapeño pepper, chopped

Directions

Drain and rinse beans. Place beans and all other ingredients in the slow-cooker and cook on LOW for 8 to 10 hours. Serve with Crockin' Cornbread or garlic bread, finely chopped red onion, and/or fresh salsa.

Submitted by Cindy Quinlan

Sides

Corn in the Crock

No matter if you serve it on a buffet spread or pass it at the table, we predict this dish will become your family's favorite side.

Ingredients

2 cans corn, drained

1 (8-ounce) block cream cheese, cubed

¼ cup sour cream

3 tablespoons butter,

¼ cup sugar

¼ cup milk

1 cup sharp cheddar cheese, shredded

Directions

Add all ingredients to the crock except for cheddar cheese. Cover and cook on LOW for 2 hours. Stir, and add cheddar cheese to corn. Cover and cook until cheese is melted.

Sides

Green Beans and Smoked Sausage

This bean-and-sausage combo is a match made in slow-cooker heaven!

Ingredients

5 medium potatoes, chopped (add more if your prefer)

2 packages smoked sausage links, sliced

1 small onion, diced

2 cloves garlic, minced (optional)

salt and pepper, to taste

3 large cans green beans, undrained

1 cup water

Directions

Place potatoes on the bottom of a 6-to 7-quart slow-cooker. Add smoked sausage slices, onion, salt and pepper, and garlic. Add green beans with juice to the slow-cooker. Add water. Cover and cook on HIGH for 6 hours.

Submitted by Janet Micheal-Hamilton

Mac and Cheese, Please!

Ingredients

2 cups macaroni, uncooked

2 tablespoons butter

1 small block Velveeta cheese

1 cup shredded cheddar cheese, divided

½ cups milk

½ block cream cheese

salt and pepper, to taste

Directions

Cook macaroni according to package directions, drain, and add to the crock. Add remaining ingredients except for the cheddar cheese. Cook on LOW for 2 hours. Top with cheddar cheese and cook until melted.

Sweet as Pie Sweet Potatoes

Just as yummy as can be, this uncomplicated dish is as easy as, well, you know!

Ingredients

6 large sweet potatoes, cubed

1 cup white sugar

2 eggs, beaten

½ cup milk

½ teaspoon salt

⅓ cup butter, melted

1 teaspoon vanilla extract

Topping

1 cup packed brown sugar

½ cup all-purpose flour

⅓ cup butter, melted

1 cup pecans, finely chopped

Directions

Cut up sweet potatoes into cubes and add to the slow-cooker. Pour sugar, beaten eggs, milk, salt, butter, and vanilla over the potatoes; mix together. Cook on HIGH for 3 hours. Open lid and mash the potatoes. In another bowl, combine the brown sugar, flour, butter, and pecans. Sprinkle on top of the mashed sweet potatoes. Cover and cook on HIGH for 1 hour.

Submitted by Dannette Woodard

All-Day Mac and Cheese

From sunup to sundown, your crew will beg to chow on this multi-tasking treat.

Ingredients

8 ounces elbow macaroni

4 cups shredded sharp cheddar cheese, divided

1 (12-ounce) can evaporated milk

1 ½ cups milk

2 eggs

1 ½ teaspoons salt

½ teaspoon pepper

Directions

In a large pot, cook the macaroni in boiling water 10 minutes, or until done; drain. In a large bowl, mix the cooked macaroni, 3 cups cheddar cheese, evaporated milk, milk, eggs, and salt and pepper. Transfer to a slow-cooker coated with non-stick cooking spray. Sprinkle with the remaining 1 cup cheddar cheese. Cover and cook on LOW for 5 to 6 hours, or until the mixture is firm and golden around the edges. Do not remove the cover or stir the mixture until it has finished cooking.

Submitted by *Wendy H. Linney*

Truckers' Beans

Drivers love the convenience of slow cookin' when they're truckin', and busy families will enjoy how effortless this is, not to mention delicious!

Ingredients

1 to 2 pounds ground beef

1 large sweet onion, chopped

1 can pinto beans, drained

1 can lima beans, drained

1 can Northern beans, drained

1 can kidney beans, drained

1 can butter beans, drained

1 can navy beans, drained

1 can baked beans, undrained

1 can diced tomatoes with green chiles

½ cup brown sugar

1 cup ketchup

1 cup barbecue sauce

1 tablespoon mustard

Directions

Cook ground beef and onion until brown. Add all ingredients to the slow-cooker and mix well. Cook on HIGH for about 4 hours. This makes a large amount and can be frozen for later.

Submitted by Floyce Cleghorn

Ranch Potatoes

Ingredients

1 bag frozen hash browns

1 block cream cheese

1 package ranch dressing mix

Directions

Put all the ingredients in the slow-cooker and cook on LOW for 3 to 6 hours.

Submitted by *Brandee Lewis*

Creamy Hash Browns

These definitely aren't your usual hash browns. And the taste? Wow!

Ingredients

2-pound package frozen, cubed hash browns

2 cups American or cheddar cheese, cubed or shredded

1 pint sour cream

1 can cream of chicken soup

½ pound sliced bacon, cooked and crumbled

Onion, chopped (amount to your liking)

¼ cup butter, melted

¼ teaspoon pepper

Directions

Place potatoes in the slow-cooker. Combine remaining ingredients and pour over potatoes. Mix well. Cover and cook on LOW for 4 to 5 hours, or until potatoes are tender.

Submitted by Lynda Kauffman

Cheddar Spirals

Give it a whirl! Just throw in whatever leftover meat you find in the fridge and you've got a kid-friendly feast.

Ingredients

16 ounces spiral-shaped pasta

2 cups half-and-half

1 can cheddar cheese soup

4 cups shredded cheddar cheese

1 to 2 cups leftover meat of your choice

Directions

Cook pasta and drain. Combine half-and-half and soup; stir in pasta, cheese, and your choice of meat. Place in the slow-cooker and cook on LOW for 2½ hours.

Submitted by Debra Allgyer

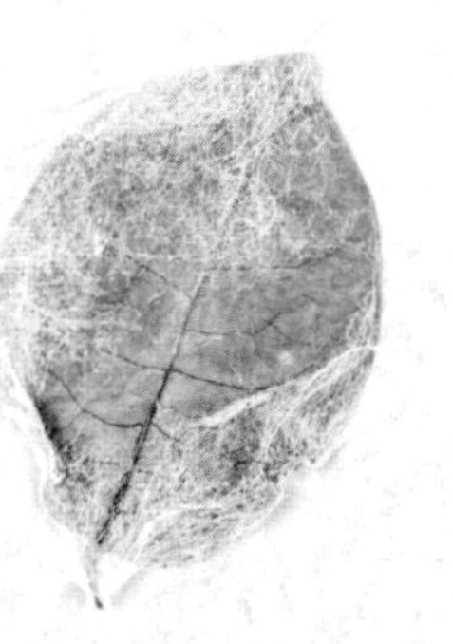

The Main Squeeze

What's for dinner? Say goodbye to the panic that rises when you hear that question while thinking to yourself, "I have NO clue!" No matter whom you're trying to please, the answer is right here in this chapter. We have a great variety of chicken, beef and pork recipes that won't make you sweat in the kitchen trying to follow the directions (because that ain't pretty). Start with our fan favorite, Teriyaki Chicken, then cook your way through the pages and you'll always know what's for dinner.

Beef

Stone Family Roast

A classic Sunday special from Jenna's childhood!

Ingredients

½ cup flour (or enough to coat roast)

salt and pepper, to taste

3 to 4-pound beef roast

1-pound package baby carrots

1 white onion, cut in rings

3 potatoes, cut in chunks

1 ½ cups beef broth

1 ½ cup water

Directions

Mix ½ cup flour with salt and pepper. Coat roast in mixture and brown in a skillet. Place in the slow-cooker with carrots, onions, and potatoes. Add beef broth and water. Cover and cook on LOW for 8 to 10 hours.

From *Jenna's mom's kitchen*

Poppy's Pot Meat

Jenna's father-in-law outdid himself with this spicy, saucy, carnivore-friendly feast, which is a Marwitz family favorite lovingly converted for the slow-cooker.

Ingredients

5 pounds beef roast, cut into 1-inch pieces

½ onion, coarsely chopped

2 cups water

Sauce

½ cup mustard

1 cup ketchup

1 tablespoon Louisiana hot sauce

1 ounce liquid smoke

½ cup brown sugar

⅔ cup Worcestershire sauce

salt and pepper, to taste

Directions

Put a layer of meat in the bottom of the slow-cooker, followed by onion and salt and pepper. Continue the layers until meat and onion are gone. Add 2 cups of water and cook on HIGH for 4 hours, stirring at about 2 hours. Dip out all but ½ inch of the juice from the slow cooker. Mix sauce ingredients and add to the meat. Stir well and cook on LOW for an additional hour.

Yaya's Roast

Nothin' beats Mama's cookin'.

Ingredients

3 to 4 pound beef roast

salt and pepper, to taste

2 teaspoons beef bouillon granules

4 potatoes, peeled and cubed

1 small package baby carrots

1 onion, cut in thick chunks

½ cup of water

Gravy

use one of the following:

cream of mushroom soup

onion soup mix

Directions

Salt and pepper roast on both sides and place in the slow-cooker. Sprinkle roast with beef granules. Put potatoes, carrots, and onion around roast and pour water over all. Cook on LOW for approximately 6 to 8 hours. After roast is done, remove roast and vegetables and make gravy by adding cream of mushroom or onion soup mix to the juice

From Nicole's mom's kitchen

Tula's Carne Guisada

Leave it to Aunt Tula to whip up this scrumptious dish served in burritos.

Ingredients

2 to 3 pounds stew meat

1 onion, cut into large chunks

½ bell pepper, chunked (or more if you like bell pepper)

2 or 3 cloves garlic, minced

flour for dredging meat

1 to 2 cans beef broth

3 to 4 tablespoons carne guisada seasoning

refried beans

flour tortillas

Directions

Dredge meat, onion, pepper, and garlic in flour until well coated. Place them all in the slow-cooker. Mix 1 can of broth and carne guisada seasoning; pour over meat mixture. Add second can of broth, if needed. (Meat should be barely covered.) Cook on LOW 7 to 10 hours. Stir at 7 hours to make sure the meat is not stuck together. (Tula cooks hers for 10 hours to get it really tender.) Serve with refried beans on flour tortillas, or dice about 4 potatoes, place in cooker with all other ingredients, and eat like a stew.

From Nicole's aunt's kitchen

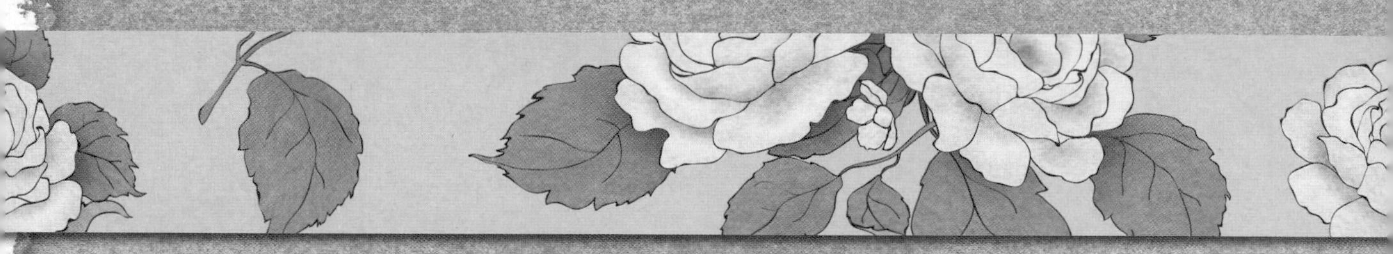

Nicole's Beef Tips

Nicole's crew is eatin' good when this hearty dish is served hot and ready.

Ingredients

- 1 pound stew meat
- flour (for dusting the meat)
- ½ cup chopped onion
- 1 teaspoon garlic powder
- 1 teaspoon salt
- ¼ teaspoon pepper
- 1 small can sliced mushrooms, drained (optional)
- 1 can cream of chicken or cream of mushroom soup
- ½ soup can water

Directions

Lightly flour the stew meat and place in the slow-cooker. Sprinkle with onion, garlic powder, salt, pepper, and mushrooms. Stir in soup and water. Cover and cook on LOW for 6 to 8 hours. If the mixture is too thin, stir approximately 3 to 4 tablespoons flour into ½ to 1 cup water until smooth. Turn up the slow-cooker to HIGH; pour the flour/water mixture through a strainer over the slow-cooker, adding a little at a time while constantly stirring the beef tips until the desired thickness is reached. Serve over rice or noodles.

From Nicole's mom's kitchen

CiCi's Crockin' Roast

As a mama of three boys, CiCi knows this hearty dish will keep bellies full.

Ingredients

3 to 4 pound boneless roast

1 tablespoon chili powder (to coat roast)

1 medium onion, chopped

1 cup dry pinto beans

2 cans diced tomatoes with green chiles

1 can cream of mushroom soup

1 can green chiles

½ teaspoon oregano

1 cup water

flour tortillas

salt and pepper, to taste

Directions

Coat roast with chili powder, then add it and the remaining ingredients to the slow-cooker. Cook on LOW for 10 to 12 hours. Stir after cooking and serve with flour tortillas.

From *Jenna's mother-in-law's kitchen*

Jenna's Beef Tips

A Crockin' Girl standby, this flavor-packed recipe makes regular appearances at Jenna's Texas home.

Ingredients

- 1 can golden mushroom soup
- ½ can water (use can from soup)
- ½ can white cooking wine (use can from soup)
- 1 packet onion soup mix
- 1 clove garlic, minced
- 1 medium onion, cut into rings
- sirloin tip steaks (2 to 3 steaks)

Directions

Combine soup, water, cooking wine, onion soup mix, and minced garlic in the slow-cooker. Whisk together to remove lumps, then add onions and steaks. (We put the steaks into the liquid whole and pull apart the meat once it is cooked; you can cut up the meat before cooking, if desired.) Make sure the steaks are fully covered in the mixture; add a little liquid to cover them, if needed. Cook LOW for 6 to 8 hours or HIGH for 3 to 4 hours.

Hungarian Goulash

Leanne's dad used to make this traditional Hungarian stew for family birthdays. We love recipes with a cool history behind them!

Ingredients

- 2 pounds round steak
- 1 onion, chopped
- 1 garlic clove, minced (add more, if desired)
- 2 tablespoons flour
- 1 teaspoon salt
- ½ teaspoon pepper
- ½ teaspoon paprika
- ¼ teaspoon dried thyme, crushed
- 1 bay leaf
- 1 can or 1 quart canned tomatoes
- 1 cup sour cream

Directions

Chop tenderized round steak into bite-sized pieces. Mix together all ingredients except sour cream. Cook on LOW for 8 to 10 hours or on HIGH for 4 to 5 hours. Remove bay leaf. Add sour cream 30 minutes before eating. Serve over buttered noodles or rice. (Leanne prefers rice because it soaks up the gravy so nicely.)

Submitted by Leanne Hicks

Hickory Smoked Brisket

Ingredients

- 3 to 4 pound beef brisket
- ¼ cup liquid smoke
- ½ teaspoon celery salt
- ½ teaspoon garlic salt
- ½ teaspoon onion powder

Directions

Place beef on a piece of foil. Sprinkle with remaining ingredients. Wrap foil securely around beef. Place in the slow-cooker, cover, and cook on LOW for 8 to 12 hours. Serve warm with juice ladled over the top.

Submitted by Barbara Schweiger

Beef and Noodles

Ingredients

2 pounds cubed stew meat

flour, for dusting cubed meat

1 tablespoon oil

1 packet onion soup mix

1 can golden mushroom soup

1 can cream of celery soup

½ cup water or ½ cup red wine (optional)

1 package noodles, cooked

Directions

In a large skillet, brown floured, cubed beef in 1 tablespoon oil. Place beef in the slow-cooker. Combine the soups and the water/wine (your preference), and onion soup mix; pour over the beef. Cook on HIGH for 4 hours or on LOW for 6 to 8 hours. Serve over cooked noodles.

Submitted by *Cathy Burris*

Peppie and Pop's Cabbage Tamales

Peppie and Pop pay loving tribute to Jenna's beloved Grammy with this slow cookin' version of her much-adored recipe.

Ingredients

1 pound ground beef

⅓ to ½ pound hot breakfast sausage

1 cup long-grain rice

5 to 6 cloves garlic, minced or chopped, and divided

1 head green cabbage

2 small cans tomato sauce

5 cans water

3 tablespoons chili blend seasoning (not chili powder; available in a jar with seasonings)

Directions

In a bowl, mix ground beef, sausage, rice, and 2 or 3 minced or chopped garlic cloves. Cut core out of cabbage and put cabbage in hot water. Pull leaves off as they get a little tender. Place meat mixture in leaves; roll up and put a toothpick in each roll. In a separate bowl, mix tomato sauce with 5 cans water, chili blend, and 2 to 3 cloves of minced or chopped garlic. Mix well. Put cabbage rolls in slow cooker, placing the least tender ones on the bottom. Then pour tomato sauce mixture over rolls, covering all. Cook on HIGH for approximately 6 hours.

From Grammy's kitchen

Crockin' Enchilada Casserole

Ingredients

1 pound hamburger meat, browned

1 can cream of chicken soup

1 can diced tomatoes with green chilies

1 can Ranch Style beans

flour tortillas

1 bag shredded Velveeta crumbles

Directions

Brown hamburger meat; add soup, tomatoes, and beans to the hamburger meat and mix well. Tear tortillas into strips and place a layer in the bottom of the slow-cooker. Next, add 1 layer of ½ the meat mixture, then a layer of cheese. Repeat layers, ending with cheese. Cook on HIGH for 3 hours.

Barbecue Beef Sandwiches
with Onion Rings and Cheese

Ingredients

- 3 pounds boneless chuck roast
- 1 ½ cups ketchup
- ¼ cup brown sugar
- ¼ cup apple cider vinegar
- 2 tablespoons mustard
- 2 tablespoons Worcestershire sauce
- 1 teaspoon liquid smoke
- ½ teaspoon salt
- ¼ teaspoon pepper
- onion rings
- shredded cheese
- buns for serving

Directions

Place roast in the slow-cooker. Combine all other ingredients except for onion rings, cheese, and buns. Pour over the roast. Cover and cook on HIGH for 4 to 5 hours or on LOW for 8 to 10 hours. Shred meat with forks. Spoon onto bottom of bun, sprinkle with cheese, top with onion rings, and cover with bun.

Submitted By *Kristi Ferguson*

Salisbury Steak

Beef patties and gravy in the slow-cooker? Yes, please!

Ingredients

2 pounds lean ground beef

1 packet onion mushroom soup mix

½ cup crushed saltine crackers

1 egg

¼ cup milk

2 tablespoons vegetable oil

¼ cup flour

2 cans cream of mushroom soup

1 packet brown gravy mix

Directions

In a large bowl, mix together the beef, onion mushroom soup mix, crushed saltine crackers, egg, and milk. Using your hands, shape beef mixture into 8 patties. Heat the oil in a large skillet over medium-high heat. Dredge the patties in flour just to coat and brown on both sides. Place the browned patties into the slow cooker (overlapping is okay). In a medium bowl, prepare the brown gravy according to package instructions. Mix in both cans of mushroom soup; pour gravy mixture over the patties. Cook on LOW for 4 to 6 hours, or until beef is done.

Mom's Italian Beef

The tang of the jarred peppers mingled with the robust Italian spices will transport you to Italy and back.

Ingredients

1 sirloin-tip roast (size depends on the amount of people you will be feeding)

1 package Italian seasoning

1 (12-ounce) can beer

2 jars pepperoncini (using only the juice from the second jar, if desired)

Directions

Place roast in the slow-cooker. Pour beer over the roast and sprinkle Italian seasoning on top. Pour in one jar of peppers and juice. Cook on LOW for 8 to 10 hours, or until beef falls apart. A few hours before serving, add juice from second jar of peppers. (You can add the peppers as well, but it will make the beef extremely spicy.) Serve with fresh roll-type bread.

Submitted by Lisa Courter

Enchiladas

Ingredients

2 pounds cooked taco meat, divided in half (hamburger meat seasoned with taco seasoning and cumin)

1 family-size cream of mushroom soup

1 regular can nacho cheese soup

1 regular can fiesta cheese soup

2 cans diced tomatoes with green chiles

1 can diced green chiles

1 large can enchilada sauce

1 medium onion, diced

flour or corn tortillas

Directions (Enchilada Sauce)

Combine half of the taco meat (1 pound) with cream of mushroom soup, nacho cheese soup, fiesta cheese soup, 1 can of diced tomatoes with green chiles, diced green chiles, enchilada sauce, and onion in the slow-cooker. Cook on HIGH for 3 hours. Great for serving as a dip or for topping enchiladas.

Directions (Enchiladas)

Keep 1 pound of seasoned taco meat in the skillet and add 1 can of diced tomatoes with green chiles. Heat thoroughly. Spoon taco mixture into tortillas of choice and roll. Top with enchilada sauce.

Submitted by Holly Ellis

Coke Roast

A can of cola is the secret to this scrumptious creation, which pops with fabulous flavor!

Ingredients

1 onion, diced

3 cloves garlic, minced

1 can golden mushroom soup

1 package onion soup mix

3 to 4 pound rump roast

olive oil, for browning roast

½ can dark soda

1 cup sour cream

Directions

Mix onion, garlic, golden mushroom soup, and onion soup mix. Pour over the roast. Next add soda, cover, and cook on LOW for 6 hours. Remove roast and slice. Add sour cream to liquid and whisk until mixed. Return the roast to the slow-cooker and cook another hour on HIGH.

French Dip Sandwiches

Kids of all ages (and that includes the adult ones, too!) will love dunking these wonderful 'wiches in the beefy juice.

Ingredients

- 2 to 3 pound pot roast
- 1 can beef broth
- 1 can beef consumé
- 1 can French onion soup
- rolls (any kind you like)
- cheese of your choice: swiss, mozzarella, or provolone

Directions

Cut the roast into big chunks. Put all ingredients in the slow-cooker; cook on LOW for 8 to 10 hours. After about 8 hours, use spoon to shred the meat. Spoon meat into rolls, top with cheese, and serve with beef juice.

Submitted by Jennifer Ritzer

Main Dish (Beef)

Roast with a Twist

Ingredients

- 3-pound roast
- 1 can golden mushroom soup
- 1 can cream of mushroom soup
- 1 pound green beans
- 1 onion, sliced or diced
- salt and pepper, to taste

Directions

Combine all ingredients in a slow-cooker. Cook on LOW for 6 to 8 hours.

Submitted by *Emily Carr*

Ground Beef Chow Mein

Your family will chow down on this Chinese-inspired dish, which easily serves eight and makes a distinctive addition to your weekly menu plan.

Ingredients

1 pound ground beef

1 medium onion, chopped

1 bunch celery, sliced

1 (28-ounce) can chop suey vegetables, drained

2 packets brown gravy mix

2 tablespoons soy sauce

hot cooked rice

3 to 4 green onions, chopped or diced

Directions

In a large skillet, cook beef and onion over medium heat until meat is no longer pink; drain and transfer to slow-cooker. Stir in the celery, chop suey vegetables, gravy mixes, and soy sauce. Cover and cook on LOW for 4 to 6 hours, or until celery is tender, stirring occasionally. Serve over rice and garnish with chopped or diced green onions.

Submitted by Judith Erva

Barbecue Beef Sliders

Two types of barbecue sauce and a bottle of beer are the main components in these crowd-pleasing sliders.

Ingredients

3 pounds chuck roast

salt, pepper, and garlic powder, to taste

1 large bottle sweet and spicy chipotle barbecue sauce

1 (12-ounce) bottle beer

1 small bottle barbecue sauce

slider buns

coleslaw

Directions

Spray slow-cooker with nonstick cooking spray. Rub the chuck roast generously on all sides with salt, pepper, and garlic powder. Place the roast in the slow-cooker. Pour on the sweet and spicy chipotle barbecue sauce to cover completely. Pour beer over the top and around the sides of the roast. Cover and cook on LOW for 7 to 8 hours, or until the roast is falling apart. Remove roast and discard all liquids. Shred beef with forks and place back in the slow-cooker. Pour in the barbecue sauce and stir to coat the meat. Set the slow cooker to LOW for 1 to 2 hours, or until time to eat. Serve on slider buns. Top with coleslaw, if desired.

Submitted by Jenn Hedrick

Swiss Steak

The slow-cooker takes what's commonly a tough cut of meat and makes it fall-off-the-fork tender.

Ingredients

2 pounds round steak

salt and pepper, to taste

1 egg, beaten

Italian bread crumbs, for coating

oil, for browning

1 large can petite chopped tomatoes

1 cup mozzarella cheese

cooked rice or mashed potatoes (optional)

Directions

Cut round steak into serving-size pieces; salt and pepper to taste. Dredge meat in egg and then coat with Italian bread crumbs. Place in skillet with ¼-inch preheated oil. Brown on both sides. Place meat into slow cooker. Pour tomatoes over meat and cook on HIGH 4 to 5 hours or on LOW for 7 to 8 hours. Thirty minutes before serving, sprinkle cheese over the meat mixture. Serve with rice or mashed potatoes.

Submitted by Kathleen Bromwich

London Broil

Ingredients

1 London broil

1 can cream of mushroom soup

1 can tomato soup

1 packet dry onion soup mix

Directions

Place meat in slow-cooker. Mix together remaining ingredients and pour over the meat. Cook on LOW for 8 to 10 hours.

Submitted by *Merri Coolbaugh*

Main Dish (Beef)

Sweet and Sour Ribs

A little sweet, a little sour, and a lot of delicious perfectly sums up this stick-to-your-ribs meal.

Ingredients

2 pounds short ribs

1 cup cola

1 large can baked beans

1 large can kidney beans

2 tablespoons brown sugar

1 teaspoon red pepper

½ teaspoon garlic powder

Directions

Spray the slow-cooker with nonstick cooking spray; add the ribs. Combine remaining ingredients and pour over the ribs. Cook on LOW for 7 to 8 hours.

Submitted by Renee Young

Pepper Steak

Y'all are going to adore this yummy fusion of flavors, which tastes terrific atop a bed of rice or noodles.

Ingredients

- 1 ½ to 2 pounds beef round steak
- 2 tablespoons cooking oil
- ¼ cup soy sauce
- 1 cup onion, chopped
- 1 garlic clove, minced
- 1 teaspoon sugar
- ½ teaspoon salt
- ¼ teaspoon pepper
- ¼ teaspoon ground ginger
- 1 (16-ounce) can petite diced tomatoes, undrained
- 2 large bell peppers, cut into strips
- ½ cup cold water
- 1 tablespoon cornstarch

Directions

Cut beef into 3-inch by 1-inch strips; brown in oil in a skillet. Transfer to the slow-cooker. Combine the next 7 ingredients; pour over beef. Cover and cook on LOW for 5 to 6 hours. Add tomatoes and bell peppers; cook on LOW for at least 1 more hour. Combine the cold water and cornstarch to make a paste; stir into liquid in the slow-cooker and cook on HIGH until thickened.

Submitted by Jodie Wright

Shepherd's Pie

Ingredients

1 pound hamburger meat

1 teaspoon thyme

1 tablespoon Worcestershire sauce

1 bag frozen hash browns

1 can corn, drained and juice reserved

1 can green beans, drained and juice reserved

1 can carrots, drained and juice reserved

1 to 2 packets brown gravy mix (prepare with reserved vegetable juices)

½ box instant mashed potatoes

2 cups water

salt and pepper, to taste

Directions

Place uncooked meat, seasonings, and Worcestershire sauce in the slow cooker; pat down ingredients. Add hash browns, vegetables, and gravy. In a bowl, mix instant potatoes with water; spread on top. Cook on HIGH for 4 hours or on LOW for 7 to 8 hours.

Submitted by Jessica Beam

Little Meats and Gravy

Kathy's family invented this recipe, which has been a favorite for many years.

Ingredients

2 pounds chuck or stew beef, cut into ½-inch pieces

1 package onion soup mix

2 cans low-sodium cream of chicken soup

2 soup cans water

cooked noodles, rice, or potatoes for serving

Directions

Combine all ingredients in the slow-cooker; stir. Cover and cook on LOW for 8 to 10 hours or on HIGH for 5 to 6 hours. Thicken, if desired, and serve over noodles, rice, or potatoes.

Submitted by *Kathy Terian*

Poultry

Teriyaki Chicken

Ingredients

1 small bag baby carrots

1 (20-ounce) can chunked pineapple

½ large red onion, cut into chunks

2 cloves garlic, minced

4 chicken breasts or 6 thighs

½ cup teriyaki sauce

salt and pepper, to taste

Directions

Layer carrots, pineapple, garlic, and onion, then add the chicken on top. Drizzle teriyaki sauce over the chicken; add salt and pepper, to taste. Cook on HIGH for 4 hours or on LOW for 6 to 8 hours.

Chicken Pot Pie

Because there's nothing better than a one-dish meal loaded with veggies to serve to your family, this is definitely Nicole's go-to dish!

Ingredients

1 whole chicken, boiled, and deboned

½ to 1 cup onion, diced

1 cup celery, diced

1 cup carrots, thinly sliced

1 cup frozen sweet peas

1 can sweet corn, drained

1 to 2 potatoes, peeled and cubed

2 tablespoons margarine

½ cup chicken broth

1 can cream of chicken soup

salt and pepper, to taste

¼ to ½ cup half-and-half (substitute with milk, if desired)

½ teaspoon salt

Dash pepper

1 package crescent rolls

Directions

Place chicken, onion, celery, carrots, peas, corn, potatoes, margarine, chicken broth, and soup in the slow-cooker; salt and pepper to taste and mix well. Cook on HIGH for 2 hours. Stir in half-and-half. Roll out crescent rolls and place on top of chicken mixture. Cook on HIGH for another hour, or until crescents are fully cooked.

Jaci's Caribbean Chicken

You'll channel the islands with this jerk-infused dish, which is the optimum combination of spicy and sweet.

Ingredients

- 4 frozen chicken breasts
- 1 ½ cups water
- 1 bottle Caribbean jerk marinade
- 1 small onion, sliced
- 1 can pineapple chunks, drained

Directions

Place chicken breasts, water, marinade, and onion in the slow-cooker. Cook on LOW 7 to 8 hours or on HIGH for 3 to 4 hours. Add pineapple chunks in the last hour or wait until the end for a fresher taste. Serve over rice or in a warm corn tortilla with pico de gallo.

From Jenna's sister's kitchen

Main Dish (Poultry)

Zesty Shredded Chicken Barbecue

Wonderful as a sandwich filling, this saucy standout gets extra zip from a big splash of Italian dressing.

Ingredients

6 boneless, skinless chicken breasts, frozen

1 (12-ounce) bottle barbecue sauce (flavor of your choice)

½ cup Italian salad dressing

¼ cup brown sugar

2 tablespoons Worcestershire sauce

1 or 2 onions, sliced

Sandwich/sub rolls, toasted

Directions

Place frozen chicken in slow-cooker (stacking is fine). In a bowl, mix together the barbecue sauce, Italian dressing, brown sugar, and Worcestershire sauce; then pour over the frozen chicken. Slice desired amount of onion and add to the slow-cooker. Cover and cook on LOW for approximately 4 hours. Remove chicken and shred with two forks, then return the shredded chicken to the slow-cooker. Cook on LOW for an additional 1 to 2 hours to soak up the sauce. Add the shredded chicken and onions to the toasted rolls.

Submitted by Amy Topola

Parmesan Chicken

Ingredients

1 packet onion soup mix
1 cup uncooked white rice
2 cups Parmesan cheese, grated and divided
1½ cups milk
2 cans cream of mushroom soup
6 boneless, skinless chicken breasts
6 tablespoons butter
salt and pepper, to taste

Directions

Mix together onion soup mix, rice, 1 cup Parmesan cheese, milk, and soup in a medium bowl. Coat slow-cooker with non-stick cooking spray. Lay chicken breasts on the bottom and place 1 tablespoon butter on top of each one. Pour soup mixture over chicken; add salt and pepper, to taste. Cook on LOW for 8 to 10 hours or on HIGH for 4 to 6 hours.

Submitted by Jamie Baumann

Best Whole Chicken

So moist, so mouthwatering, so packed with yum . . . this honestly is the best bird we've tasted in a long time.

Ingredients

2 teaspoons paprika
1 teaspoon salt
1 teaspoon onion powder
1 teaspoon thyme
½ teaspoon garlic powder
¼ teaspoon cayenne pepper
¼ teaspoon black pepper
1 onion, loosely chopped
1 large chicken

Directions

Combine the dried spices in a small bowl. Place onion in the bottom of the slow-cooker. Remove any giblets from the chicken, then rub all over with the spice mixture. You can even put some spices inside the cavity and under the skin covering the breasts. Put prepared chicken on the onions in the slow-cooker, cover it, and cook on HIGH for 4 to 5 hours (for a 3- to 4-pound chicken), or until the chicken is falling off the bone.

Submitted by Danielle Ryan

Chicken in a Hurry

Yes, indeed. This recipe surely does live it up its name!

Ingredients

2 ½ to 3 pounds drumsticks
½ cup ketchup
¼ cup water
¼ cup brown sugar, packed
1 packet onion soup mix

Directions

Arrange chicken in the slow-cooker. Combine remaining ingredients and then pour over the chicken. Cover and cook on HIGH for 4 to 5 hours or on LOW for 7 to 8 hours.

Submitted by Josee Garceau

Kari's Rotisserie Deli-Style Chicken

Ingredients

- 3 to 4 pound whole chicken
- olive oil or non-stick cooking spray
- seasoned salt
- garlic powder or lemon pepper, to taste

Directions

Rinse chicken inside and out, then spray lightly with cooking spray or rub lightly with olive oil. Sprinkle inside and outside with seasoned salt, as well as with your choice of garlic powder or lemon pepper. Ball foil into 4 (2- to 3-inch) balls and place them in the bottom of the slow-cooker to keep the chicken elevated. Place chicken, breast side down, on top of foil balls. Cook on HIGH for approximately 5 hours. Check with a meat thermometer to make sure chicken is cooked thoroughly.

Submitted by Kari Wiant

Cranberry Chicken

Crockin' Girls love the color of this pretty poultry dish, which is divine over egg noodles or rice.

Ingredients

4 to 6 boneless, skinless chicken breasts

1 can whole cranberries

1 (16-ounce) bottle Russian dressing

1 packet onion soup mix

Directions

Spray inside of slow-cooker with non-stick cooking spray. Place chicken in the bottom of the slow-cooker. Mix together cranberries, dressing, and soup mix; pour over chicken. Cook on LOW for 6 to 7 hours or on HIGH for 3 to 4 hours.

Submitted by Mary Grace McAlevy

Soul Food Cream of Chicken

This is home-cookin' the way it should be: no fuss, no muss . . . just full-on delish.

Ingredients

1 whole fryer, cut up

1 yellow onion

salt, pepper, celery salt, and garlic salt, to taste

2 cans cream of mushroom soup

1 can chicken broth

bella mushrooms to your liking

Directions

Place sliced onion and mushrooms in the slow-cooker. Place cut-up fryer on top and add salt, pepper, celery salt, and garlic salt. Combine soup with chicken broth, then pour over chicken evenly. Cover and cook on LOW for 8 hours or on HIGH for 4 to 5 hours. Serve with rice.

Submitted by Lenora Fleming

Salsa Chicken

Solve your what's-for-dinner dilemma in a snap with this two-ingredient recipe, which pairs well with Spanish rice, warm tortillas, or even on top of a baked potato!

Ingredients

4 frozen boneless, skinless chicken breasts

1 large jar salsa (your choice)

Directions

Combine ingredients in the slow-cooker. Cook on LOW for 6 to 8 hours or on HIGH for 4 to 6 hours. Shred the chicken and stir together with the salsa broth.

Submitted by Geneva Harvison

Creamy Apricot Chicken

Not only does this taste amazing, but it looks so pretty on the plate, too!

Ingredients

1 (8-ounce) bottle Russian or creamy French salad dressing

1 (12-ounce) jar apricot preserves

1 to 2 pounds boneless, skinless chicken breasts

Directions

Combine salad dressing and preserves. Place chicken in the slow-cooker and pour dressing mixture on top. Cover and cook on LOW for 4 to 5 hours. Serve over rice, noodles, or mashed potatoes.

Submitted by Michelle Navoney

Golden Mushroom Chicken

We're gaga for this gold-standard dish, which features white wine and sliced 'shrooms.

Ingredients

4 chicken breasts

½ cup white wine

1 can golden mushroom soup

1 package cream cheese with chives

1 package sliced mushrooms

¼ cup butter

Directions

Place chicken in the slow-cooker and pour wine over it. Combine soup and cream cheese; pour over chicken. Top with mushrooms and butter. Cook on LOW for 5 hours. Serve over angel hair pasta or rice.

Submitted by Mary Lou Chiles

Southwestern Chicken Lasagna

One thing we adore about slow-cooking is that it gives you the freedom to take a classic recipe and make it your own. This one is no exception!

Ingredients

2 large cooked chicken breasts, shredded

1 (14-ounce) bag frozen Southwest-blend vegetables

1 bag tortilla chips, crushed

1 (28-ounce) can red enchilada sauce

6 ounces shredded extra-sharp cheddar cheese

Directions

In the bottom of the slow-cooker, layer chicken, vegetables, and crushed tortilla chips; repeat layers finishing with chips. Drizzle entire can of enchilada sauce over the lasagna and cover with shredded cheese. Cook on HIGH for 5 hours.

Submitted by Linda Hull

Polynesian Chicken

Treat the entire family to a taste of the islands with this pineapple-poultry combination.

Ingredients

4 to 6 boneless, skinless chicken breasts

1 cup brown sugar

½ cup soy sauce

1 (16-ounce) can pineapple chunks

Directions

Place chicken in the slow-cooker. Mix together remaining ingredients and pour over the chicken. Cover and cook on LOW for 6 to 8 hours. Serve with rice.

Submitted by Arleen Dellentas

Lemon Pepper Turkey Breast

Ingredients

4 to 5 pound turkey breast, frozen or thawed

1 large onion, diced

3 stalks celery, diced

½ cup butter, melted

salt, to taste

lemon pepper seasoning, to taste

1 (14-ounce) can chicken broth

Directions

Defrost turkey (if frozen) and rinse in cool water. Pat dry. Put onion and celery in slow-cooker; place turkey breast upright over the veggies. Pour the melted butter over the turkey breast, then sprinkle with salt and lemon pepper seasoning, to taste. Pour the broth around the turkey (not over the top; you don't want to rinse the seasonings off the turkey); cover. Cook on HIGH for 6 to 7 hours.

Submitted by *Cindi Hatch*

Russell's Barbecue Stuffed Chicken

Have your beverage ready because the heat is on in this spicy, saucy supper!

Ingredients

- 4 chicken breasts
- 1 pound bacon, cooked and chopped
- ½ sliced bell pepper
- ½ bunch cilantro, chopped
- 1 ½ cups shredded cheddar cheese
- ⅓ cup pickled jalapeños, diced
- 3 cups barbecue sauce

Directions

In a bowl, mix all ingredients except chicken and barbecue sauce. Butterfly chicken breasts and stuff with half of the mixture. Fold over the chicken breasts and press along the edges to seal. Place breasts in the slow-cooker, cover with barbecue sauce, and sprinkle with the other half of the mixture. Cover and cook on LOW for 4 to 6 hours.

Submitted by Russell Parr

Dad's Chicken

Jill's daddy made this for her and her siblings when they were kiddos.

Ingredients

- 6 to 8 boneless, skinless chicken breasts
- 2 cans cream of chicken soup
- 2 cans cream of potato soup
- 1 can milk (use empty soup can to measure)
- 1 to 2 tablespoons butter
- salt and pepper, to taste
- 4 to 6 potatoes, peeled and cut into chunks

Directions

Combine soups, milk, butter, salt, and pepper in the slow-cooker. Add potatoes and chicken. Cook on HIGH for about 4 hours, or until chicken and potatoes are done.

Submitted By Jill Powell

Pork

Most Amazing Pork Chops

The name of this tasty, simple recipe truly says it all! A crowd favorite, it has circulated through our Facebook page and into many homes.

Ingredients

4 bone-in, thick-cut pork chops

1 can cream of chicken soup

1 packet onion soup mix

1 packet dry pork gravy mix

1 ½ cups chicken broth

Directions

Place the pork chops in the bottom of the slow-cooker. Mix the remaining four ingredients in a bowl, then pour over the top of the meat. Cover and cook on LOW for 6 to 8 hours.

Mandy's Big Mess

It may look like a major mess. But the taste and aroma are purely divine!

Ingredients

1 pound smoked sausage, sliced (your favorite brand)

1 bell pepper, chopped

1 purple onion, chopped

1 can pineapple chunks, drained

1 jar sweet and sour sauce

1 tablespoon Tabasco sauce (may add more, to taste)

fresh jalapeño, optional

Directions

Place all ingredients in the slow-cooker. Cook on HIGH for 1 to 1 ½ hours or on LOW for 3 to 4 hours, or until bell pepper and onion are tender. Serve atop a bed of rice or by itself with a salad.

From Jenna's sister-in-law's kitchen

Shredded Pork Loin Roast

One recipe, many meals. That's what crockin' is all about!

Ingredients

1 (5-pound) pork loin roast

onion powder, to taste

garlic powder, to taste

1 bottle barbecue sauce

1 can soda

Directions

Place roast into the slow-cooker and season with onion and garlic powder. Cover with barbecue sauce and then pour soda over the roast. Cook on LOW for 6 to 8 hours, or until pork is tender. Shred with forks.

Serving Suggestions

1. barbecue pork roast sandwiches served with lettuce, tomato, chips, and a pickle
2. barbecue pork roast loaded baked potato served with sour cream, butter, and chives
3. barbecue pork roast nachos served with chips, refried beans, lettuce, tomatoes, onion, black olives, and shredded cheese
4. barbecue pork roast corn tortilla tacos served with broccoli slaw and avocados

Ham

Yep, it's always super snappy to ham it up with your slow-cooker!

Ingredients

1 ham, pre-cooked, bone-in, spiral cut

3 cups brown sugar

1 can pineapple tidbits, undrained

Directions

Sprinkle enough brown sugar to cover the bottom of the slow-cooker. Place ham on top and pour pineapple tidbits with juice over the ham. Sprinkle more brown sugar over the top, or sprinkle the package of dry glaze that comes with the ham. Cook on LOW for 6 to 8 hours.

Pork Chop and Rice Casserole

Ingredients

4 to 6 pork chops (however many your family needs)

1 onion, sliced into rings

1 can cream mushroom soup

1 can petite diced tomatoes

1 ½ cups cooked rice of your choice

¼ cup water

salt and pepper, to taste

small amount of vegetable oil

Directions

Salt and pepper pork chops; brown in skillet with the oil. Spray slow-cooker with non-stick spray. Mix mushroom soup, diced tomatoes, and onions in the slow-cooker. Place pork chops in the mixture and cook on LOW for 4 to 6 hours. Mix in cooked rice and cook another 30 minutes, or until hot.

From Nicole's kitchen

Sausage, Potato, and Onion-Stuffed Peppers

Your family and friends will think you slaved all day in the kitchen making this gorgeous dish. (Little do they know!)

Ingredients

1 can crushed tomatoes
1 teaspoon dried oregano
¼ teaspoon each kosher salt and black pepper
1 small onion, chopped
1 to 2 small potatoes (golden or red), diced
1 cup fresh flat-leaf parsley, roughly chopped
¼ teaspoon crushed red pepper, optional
1 pound Italian sausage, casings removed
4 large bell peppers

Directions

In a 6-quart (or larger) slow-cooker, combine the tomatoes, oregano, salt, and black pepper. In a bowl, combine all ingredients except bell peppers. Mix well. Cut the stems off and discard seeds. Spoon the sausage mixture (about 1 cup each) into the peppers. Arrange the peppers upright in the slow-cooker and place the tops over the filling. Cover and cook on LOW for 5 to 6 hours or on HIGH for 3 to 4 hours, or until the sausage is cooked through and the peppers are tender. Using 2 large spoons, transfer the peppers to plates, letting any excess liquid drain into the sauce. Stir the sauce and serve with the peppers.

Submitted by Nicole Flynn

Heartthrob Pork

Tickers will go pitter-patter when you serve Paula's recipe, which is her favorite go-to for impressing guests.

Ingredients

2-pound pork tenderloin, cut into large pieces

1 can apple pie filling

1 bottle barbecue sauce

cooked rice, for serving

Directions

Place all ingredients in the slow-cooker; mix well. Cook on LOW for 8 hours. Serve with rice.

Submitted by Paula Barth

Black-Eyed Peas and Pork Chops

Ingredients

3 to 4 cans black-eyed peas

3 to 4 boneless pork chops (more can be added, if needed)

garlic powder, salt, and pepper, to taste

1 large onion, sliced

Directions

Pour the black-eyed peas in the slow-cooker; do not drain. Season pork chops however you like; Ginger uses garlic powder, salt, and pepper. Layer pork chops on top of peas and quarter onion on top. Cook on LOW about 8 hours or on HIGH for 4 hours.

Submitted by Ginger Ray

Polish Potatoes

An international twist on a standby dish, this would be perfect for a potluck—but just as fitting for a family sit-down at home.

Ingredients

1 pound Polish sausage, cut into 1-inch pieces

6 medium potatoes, peeled and quartered

3 cans golden mushroom soup

1 can water

Directions

Place sausage and potatoes in the slow-cooker. Mix soup and water and pour over potatoes. Cook on LOW for about 4 hours, or until potatoes are tender.

Submitted by Jackie Brown

Easy Pork Chops with Tomato and Garlic

Easy is the name of the game with this fuss-free recipe.

Ingredients

6 pork chops

2 large onions, sliced

4 tablespoons garlic, minced

2 cans diced tomatoes

1 ¼ cups chicken broth

1 tablespoon thyme

salt and pepper, to taste

cooked rice

Directions

Brown the pork chops on both sides in a skillet. Drain off excess fat and place in the slow-cooker. Add remaining ingredients to the pork chops; cover and cook on HIGH for 3 hours, or until very tender. If you don't love onion and garlic like we do, you can cut down on the amount. Serve with hot, cooked rice.

Submitted by Darnell Moonda Fugate

Mexican Pork Roast

Ingredients

1 pork roast (sized to fit into your slow-cooker)

1 can fat-free refried beans

1 jar picante sauce (your choice of heat)

1 package flour or corn tortillas

Optional Toppings

shredded cheese

sour cream

chopped onions

Directions

Place pork roast in the slow-cooker. Cover with refried beans and pour picante sauce over the roast. Cover and cook on LOW all day until the roast is falling apart. Shred meat with 2 forks while in the slow-cooker, mixing with the beans and picante sauce. Heat tortillas, and serve with roast and toppings.

Submitted By Gayle Pettey

Cheddar Vegetable Sausage Casserole

Ingredients

1 (10-ounce) package frozen mixed vegetables

3 large potatoes, diced

8 servings sausage, browned and sliced into pieces

1 (10-ounce) can cheddar cheese soup

1 (10-ounce) can cream of celery soup

1 cup shredded cheddar cheese

Directions

Mix all ingredients together in the slow-cooker. Cook on LOW for 6 hours.

Submitted by Michelle Mescher

Mama's Twist on Asian Pork

Don't let the amount of ingredients fool you. This is extraordinarily easy, intensely delicious, and well worth the extra dash of this and that.

Ingredients

2 large onions, thinly sliced
3 garlic cloves, minced
½ teaspoon salt
½ teaspoon pepper
1 boneless pork roast (about 3 pounds)
1 tablespoon canola oil
3 bay leaves
¼ cup hot water
¼ cup honey
¼ cup soy sauce
2 tablespoons rice vinegar
1 teaspoon ground ginger
¼ teaspoon ground cloves
3 tablespoons corn starch
¼ cup cold water
cooked rice

Directions

Place onions in the slow-cooker. In a small bowl, combine garlic, salt, and pepper. Cut roast in half; rub with garlic mixture. In a large pan, heat the canola oil and brown roast on all sides. Move the roast to the slow-cooker and add bay leaves. In a small bowl, combine hot water and honey; stir in soy sauce, vinegar, ginger, and cloves. Pour over the roast. Cover and cook on LOW for 4 to 5 hours. Remove meat and onion from the slow-cooker. Throw away bay leaves. In a bowl, combine cornstarch and cold water until smooth. Gradually stir into the slow-cooker and add pork chops and onion. Cover and cook on high for 30 minutes, or until sauce has thickened. Slice pork; top with onions and sauce. Serve with egg noodles or rice.

Submitted by Maureen Girardin

Pork Chalupas

When you're hankering for a foodie fiesta, these really hit the spot.

Ingredients

1 pound dried pinto beans

1 (3 ½-pound) bone-in pork loin roast

2 (4-ounce) cans chopped green chiles

2 garlic cloves, chopped

1 teaspoon ground cumin

1 (10-ounce) can diced tomatoes and green chilies with lime and cilantro

1 (32-ounce) box chicken broth

1 bag corn chips

Toppings

shredded Monterey Jack cheese

tomatoes

sour cream

Directions

Rinse and sort the beans according to package directions. Place beans in the slow-cooker, then add roast and next 4 ingredients. Pour chicken broth evenly over the top of the roast. Cover and cook on HIGH for 1 hour, reduce heat to LOW, and cook an additional 9 hours. Or cover and cook on HIGH for 6 hours. Remove bones and fat from roast; pull pork into large pieces with 2 forks. Cook uncovered on HIGH for 1 more hour, or until liquid is slightly thickened. Serve over corn chips with toppings.

Submitted by Teresa A. Fox

Sausage and Peppers

Ingredients

3 to 4 green or red peppers (or both)

½ onion (or more if you like)

1 package frozen Italian sausage links (use more if you have a large family)

2 cans diced tomatoes, undrained

salt, pepper, and garlic, to taste

Directions

Cut up the onions and peppers into strips; put them in the slow-cooker with the sausage links, tomatoes, and spices. Cover and cook on LOW for 6 to 8 hours. Serve over rice.

Submitted by *Georgette Ahneman*

Easy Crock Chops

Ingredients

1 can golden mushroom soup

6 (1-inch-thick) pork chops

Mixture

½ cup flour

1 teaspoon salt, seasoned salt, or your favorite seasoning

¾ teaspoon garlic powder

1 ½ teaspoons dry mustard

pepper, to taste

Directions

Brown and seer chops in oil. Dredge pork in mixture. Add to the slow-cooker. Spoon soup over each chop. Add water to remaining soup in can and pour over chops. Cook on LOW for 6 to 7 hours.

Submitted by Stephanie Baker

Red Beans and Rice

Louisiana is in the house with this big-flavored, easy-does-it one-dish dinner, which easily serves 10 to 12.

Ingredients

1 ½ pounds smoked, link sausage, cut into 2-inch pieces

4 (15-ounce) cans New Orleans red beans

1 packet onion soup mix

1 tablespoon Worcestershire sauce

1 (19-ounce) can chili

½ can of water

½ teaspoon seasoned salt

Directions

Place all ingredients in the slow-cooker. Cook on LOW for 4 to 6 hours. Serve over rice.

Submitted by Annette Wolverton

My Crock O' Ribs

Have plenty of napkins on hand to catch the drips from these lip-smackin' delights.

Ingredients

3 to 5 pounds baby back ribs (cut to fit in the slow-cooker)

1 to 2 large onions, chopped

2 cups sliced mushrooms (optional)

1 jar regular barbecue sauce

2 to 4 tablespoons chopped garlic

¾ to 1 cup brown sugar

½ cup red wine (optional)

Directions

Place ribs, onions, and mushrooms (if desired) on the bottom of the slow-cooker. Mix together barbecue sauce, garlic, brown sugar, and red wine (if desired); pour over ribs and cover. Cook on LOW for 7 to 8 hours, or on HIGH for 4 to 5 hours and then on LOW for 1 hour.

Submitted by Maggie Cerro

Spiced Pork Chops

Ingredients

1 (16-ounce) jar fruit salsa (peach, mango or pineapple)

3 tablespoons brown sugar

1 tablespoon maple syrup

2 teaspoons seafood/meat seasoning

6 boneless pork loin chops cut 1-inch thick

2 tablespoons olive oil

1 thinly sliced onion

1/2 cup orange juice

Directions

In slow-cooker, combine salsa, brown sugar, maple syrup, and seafood/meat seasoning. Trim fat from pork. Brown pork in oil in large skillet; transfer to slow-cooker. Add onion to skillet; cook until softened. Add orange juice, stirring up browned bits; pour over pork. Cover and cook on LOW for 6 to 8 hours, or until pork is tender. Spoon sauce over pork chops and serve over egg noodles.

Easy Italian Crockin'

Sit back, relax, and enjoy the finer things in life! These easy pasta dishes will ring in praises from kids and adults alike. The ingredients are easy, and the directions are simple (just the way we like it). We didn't think you could crock a pizza, but we found a way and (no lie!) it's super yummo. When we're crunched for time and resources, pastas are great go-to recipes that help us feel good about getting dinner on the table.

Pastas

Crockin' Girls Pizza

Ingredients

1 can refrigerated pizza dough
1 to 2 cups pizza sauce
1 to 2 cups mozzarella cheese
1 package Canadian bacon
1 red onion, diced
1 small can pineapple chunks, drained
1 small can black olives, drained

Directions

Spray slow-cooker with cooking spray. Place dough in the bottom of the slow-cooker, letting it come up the sides about 1 inch. Place sauce on dough; add the cheese and toppings. Cover and cook on HIGH for about 2 hours.

Pastas

Spaghetti Sauce

This slow-cookin' sauce rivals the stovetop version any day of the year. It also works beautifully in our Crockin' Lasagna.

Ingredients

1 (28-ounce) can tomato sauce

1 (6-ounce) can tomato paste

1 capful of spaghetti seasoning (you can use the packaged variety and just sprinkle over the top)

¼ cup Worcestershire sauce

¼ cup brown sugar

1 pound ground beef or turkey, browned and drained

Directions

Put all of the ingredients in the slow-cooker; mix together and simmer on LOW for 2 hours or all day, if desired. Serve over your favorite cooked pasta.

Submitted by Kelly Teeter

Crockin' Lasagna

This incredibly delicious dish is all the rage on our Facebook page, which never stops buzzing with recipe requests.

Ingredients

2 pounds ground beef
2 jars marinara sauce
2-pound tub ricotta cheese
3 to 4 cups mozzarella cheese
1 egg, beaten
1 package uncooked lasagna noodles
Italian seasoning, to taste
fresh baby spinach (2 to 3 handfuls)
non-stick cooking spray

Directions

Brown hamburger meat; drain and add marinara sauce. Let simmer for 20 minutes. (You can also make your own marinara sauce.) While simmering, in a bowl combine ricotta cheese, mozzarella cheese, egg, and Italian seasoning; mix well. Set aside 2 cups meat sauce and 1 cup cheese mixture. Spray the slow-cooker with cooking spray, and start your layers of 1) meat sauce, 2) uncooked lasagna noodles, 3) ricotta cheese mixture, and 4) spinach; repeat layers one more time. Top with remaining meat sauce and cheese. Cook on LOW for 3 hours; any longer will overcook the noodles.

White Spaghetti

We know you're going to love this creamy, dreamy pasta as much as we do. And so will your kiddos!

Ingredients

5 to 6 boneless, skinless chicken breasts

1 block cream cheese

1 package Italian seasoning

1 can cream of chicken soup

1 (16-ounce) package spaghetti noodles

Directions

Combine chicken, cream cheese, seasoning, and cream of chicken soup in the slow-cooker. Cook on LOW for 6 hours. Before serving, cook spaghetti noodles according to package directions and add to chicken mixture.

Submitted by Amanda Goben

Buffalo Chicken Pasta

Although this recipe uses inexpensive ingredients available in any grocery store, it tastes like a million bucks.

Ingredients

- 1 pound chicken breasts, chopped
- salt and pepper, to taste
- 1 can cream of chicken soup
- ½ cup hot sauce for buffalo wings (we used medium)
- 1 can diced tomatoes with green chilies, drained
- 1½ cups shredded mozzarella or cheddar cheese
- ½ cup ranch dressing
- 1½ cups sour cream
- 3 cups penne pasta, cooked

Directions

Season chicken with salt and pepper and place in the slow-cooker. Add the chicken soup, hot sauce, and diced tomatoes with green chilies; stir. Cook on LOW for 4 to 6 hours or on HIGH for 2 to 3 hours. Stir in cheese, dressing, and sour cream, then turn off the slow-cooker. Boil pasta according to package instructions; drain well and add to the slow-cooker. Stir well and serve.

Submitted by Hilary MacIsaac

Baked Ziti

If you thought cooking this awesome Italian meal was only possible in the oven, then you're in for a lip-smackin' surprise!

Ingredients

1 to 1 ¼ pounds ground beef or Italian sausage/ ground turkey (whatever suits your fancy)

1 onion, chopped

2 garlic cloves, minced

1 (15-ounce) container ricotta cheese

2 egg whites

16 ounces mozzarella cheese, divided

1 cup Parmesan cheese, divided

1 (16-ounce) box ziti noodles

2 (26-ounce) cans of spaghetti/pasta sauce

¼ teaspoon parsley

½ teaspoon oregano

Directions

Brown ground beef with the onion and garlic; drain and set aside. Combine ricotta cheese, egg whites, 8 ounces of mozzarella, Parmesan, and oregano in a separate bowl; mix well. Rinse uncooked ziti in cold water. In the slow-cooker, layer 2 cups of sauce, half of the ground beef mixture, 2 ounces mozzarella, half of the ziti, and half of the ricotta cheese mixture; repeat. Top with the remaining sauce and remaining mozzarella. Sprinkle the remaining oregano and the parsley on top. Cover and cook on LOW for 5 to 6 hours.

Submitted by Alissa Maxwell

Cheesy Chicken Spaghetti

Pasta night at your house just got a whole lot yummier, thanks to this palate-pleasing dish, which gets a hearty dose of creaminess from a pound of melted cheese.

Ingredients

- 1 pound Velveeta
- 2 cans chicken, drained and flaked
- 1 can cream of mushroom soup
- 1 can diced tomatoes with green chilies
- 1 (4-ounce) can mushroom stems and pieces, drained
- ½ cup water
- 1 small onion, diced
- 1 medium green pepper, diced
- salt and pepper, to taste
- 1 can cream of chicken soup
- 1 (12-ounce) package of spaghetti, cooked and drained

Directions

Spray the slow-cooker with non-stick cooking spray. Combine all ingredients except noodles and stir well. Cook on LOW for 2 to 3 hours, adding noodles the last 30 minutes. Stir again just before serving.

Submitted by Brenda Harris

Angel Chicken

When we took our first bite of Kari's creation, we had one word: Heavenly!

Ingredients

4 to 6 boneless, chicken breasts

¼ cup butter

½ packet dry Italian salad dressing mix

1 can cream of mushroom soup

½ cup dry white wine

4 ounces cream cheese with onions and chives

1 box penne pasta

chives, for garnish

Directions

Put all ingredients in the slow-cooker except pasta; cook on LOW for 7 to 8 hours. When the chicken mixture is done, prepare pasta according to package directions; drain. Mix pasta with chicken. Serve in a large bowl with chives sprinkled on top.

Submitted by Kari Routledge

Chicken Cacciatore

Not a fan of chicken thighs? No prob! You can swap them for boneless, skinless breasts instead.

Ingredients

1 (28-ounce) jar spaghetti sauce

1 cup onion, chopped

1 cup bell pepper, chopped

2 cloves garlic, minced

1½ to 2 pounds chicken thighs

2 tablespoons olive oil

1 (12-ounce) package rotini or penne pasta, cooked

Directions

Pour a small amount of sauce in the bottom of the slow-cooker. Briefly sauté the onion and pepper in oil with garlic; place in the slow-cooker. Lightly brown chicken pieces in the remaining oil; place on top of the onions and peppers. Pour remaining sauce over the top of the chicken. Cover and cook on LOW for 6 to 7 hours. Remove the chicken pieces, discard bones, and return chicken to the slow-cooker. (This step can be eliminated if you use boneless, skinless breasts.) Stir in the cooked pasta and heat through. Serve with Parmesan cheese.

Submitted by Carl Buehler

Our Sweet Things

The two of us and our "sweet things" LOVE us some chocolate! Which is why you'll see it used so frequently in this chapter! But chocolate is not all you'll find. There are recipes to satisfy any sweet tooth, including cobblers, cakes, brownies, and more! We enjoy making the kitchen a fun place for everyone to participate by pouring and mixing the recipes. And of course, they get to lick the spoons when we're done. Crockin' never tasted so good.

Desserts

Peanut Clusters

Guests will go gaga over these ooey, gooey crunch-tastic treats!

Ingredients

1 (16-ounce) jar unsalted peanuts

1 (16-ounce) jar salted peanuts

4 ounces German sweet chocolate

1 (12-ounce) package semisweet chocolate chips

2 pounds white almond bark (2 packages)

Directions

Place peanuts in the bottom of the slow-cooker. Place all the chocolate on top of the peanuts. Cover and cook on LOW for 3 hours. Remove lid and stir peanut mixture until chocolate is melted. Place spoonfuls of peanut mixture onto wax paper. Let cool until chocolate is hardened. Makes several dozen clusters.

Apple Crisp

You'll love our updated twist on this old-fashioned favorite, which pairs perfectly with a scoop of vanilla ice cream.

Ingredients

- 1 cup all-purpose flour
- ½ cup light brown sugar
- 1 cup white sugar, divided
- 1 teaspoon ground cinnamon, divided
- ¼ teaspoon ground nutmeg
- 1 pinch salt
- ½ cup butter (1 stick), cut into pieces
- 1 cup chopped walnuts
- 1 tablespoon cornstarch
- ½ teaspoon ground ginger
- 6 cups apples, cored and chopped (peeled, if desired)
- 2 tablespoons lemon juice

Directions

1. Mix together flour, brown sugar, ½ cup of white sugar, ½ teaspoon cinnamon, nutmeg, and salt in a bowl. Combine butter with the mixture using a fork or your fingers until coarse crumbs form. Stir in walnuts and set aside.
2. Whisk together ⅓ cup sugar, cornstarch, ginger, and ½ teaspoon cinnamon.
3. Place the apples in the bottom of the slow-cooker, then stir in the cornstarch mixture; toss with lemon juice.
4. Sprinkle the walnut crumb topping (step 1 mixture) over the top.
5. Cover and cook on HIGH for 2 hours or on LOW for 4 hours, or until apples are tender. After cooking time is complete, uncover the slow-cooker to allow the topping to harden for about an hour.

Pumpkin Crumb Cake

Ingredients

1 box cinnamon crumb cake mix (includes cake mix and cinnamon topping)

1 cup water

1 egg

1 cup canned pumpkin

1 teaspoon vanilla

1 cup white chocolate chips

½ cup chopped pecans

Directions

Mix all ingredients except chopped pecans and cinnamon topping. In a separate bowl, mix cinnamon topping with chopped pecans. Spray slow-cooker with non-stick cooking spray. Pour in half of cake mix and top with cinnamon topping/pecan mix, then repeat once more. Cover and cook on HIGH for about 2 hours, then remove lid and turn off the slow-cooker. Let the cake sit for about 15 minutes, then serve.

Fudge Brownies

So moist and chocolately, once you taste these little gems, you'll never bake brownies in the oven again!

Ingredients

1 package original brownie mix

¾ cup chocolate syrup

1 cup boiling water

1 cup chopped nuts (we used walnuts)

½ cup chocolate chips

Directions

Spray the slow-cooker with non-stick cooking spray. Prepare the brownie mix as directed on the box and pour into the slow-cooker. Mix chocolate syrup with boiling water. Pour over the brownie mix. Sprinkle with chopped nuts and chocolate chips. Cook on HIGH for 2½ to 3 hours. Turn off slow-cooker, remove lid, and let brownies sit for 15 minutes. Serve with ice cream or whipped topping and strawberries, if desired.

Kahlúa Cake

Mocha-flavored liquor merged with chocolate pudding results in one of the most sinfully rich cakes we've ever tasted!

Ingredients

1 box yellow cake mix

½ cup sugar

1 large box instant chocolate pudding

1 cup oil

4 eggs

¼ cup vodka (substitute with Kahlúa, if desired)

¼ cup Kahlúa (add this in addition to the ¼ cup Kahlúa substituted for vodka above)

¾ cup water

Icing

½ cup powdered sugar

¼ cup Kahlúa

Directions

Mix all ingredients and pour into a greased slow-cooker. Cook on HIGH for 3 hours. For icing, mix powdered sugar and Kahlúa; drizzle on top of cake.

Chocolate Lava Cake

Satisfy your sweet tooth with this rave-worthy dessert, which bursts with chocolatey goodness.

Ingredients

1 box chocolate cake mix

eggs, vegetable oil, and water (needed for cake mix)

1 small box instant chocolate pudding mix

milk for pudding

1 (12-ounce) package chocolate chips (of your choice)

Toppings (optional)

ice cream

whipped topping

nuts

Directions

Prepare cake mix according to box instructions. Pour batter into slow-cooker. Prepare pudding mix according to box instructions and pour over cake batter. Sprinkle chocolate chips on the batter. Cook on HIGH for 3 to 3½ hours. Cake will be moist and have small "lava" bubbles on top. Scoop out and serve with toppings of choice.

Donna's Brownies

Nicole's favorite! Her Nanee even mailed these to her in college.

Ingredients

1½ cups flour

2 cups sugar

½ cup cocoa

⅔ cup oleo, melted

4 eggs, well beaten

2 teaspoons vanilla

1 cup nuts, chopped (Nicole prefers pecans)

Directions

Mix together all dry ingredients, except for nuts. Melt oleo and add to the dry ingredients; mix well. Add in eggs and vanilla and then nuts. Spread in slow-cooker and cook on HIGH for 2½ to 3 hours.

From Nicole's Nanee's kitchen

Fruity Favorite

Ideal for the slow-cooker no matter the occasion, this to-die-for dessert always gets high marks.

Ingredients

1 large can crushed pineapple, drained

1 large can cherry pie filling

1 box yellow cake mix

2 sticks butter, melted

1 can angel-flake coconut

1 cup chopped pecans

Directions

Place ingredients in the slow-cooker in the order listed. Cover and cook on HIGH for 2½ to 3 hours (in a 4-quart slow-cooker), or until toothpick inserted in center comes out clean.

From Jenna's mother-in-law's kitchen

Nana's Zucchini Bread

Entertaining her family is what Nana does best. Tasty treats always await.

Ingredients

- 2 cups sugar
- 2 cups margarine
- 3 eggs
- 2 cups shredded raw zucchini
- 1 teaspoon vanilla
- 3 cups flour
- ¼ teaspoon baking powder
- 1 tablespoon baking soda
- ½ tablespoon salt
- 1 tablespoon cinnamon
- ½ teaspoon clove and allspice
- ¼ teaspoon nutmeg and ginger
- 1 cup raisins
- 1 cup walnuts
- 4 x 8-inch rectangle pan

Directions

This recipe will make two loaves of bread, but only 1 bread pan will fit into your slow-cooker. You can place extra batter in the fridge for up to 2 days. You will need an oval slow-cooker to fit a 4 x 8-inch bread pan. Blend sugar and margarine and add eggs. Mix well. Stir in the remaining ingredients. Spray the bread pan with non-stick cooking spray. Pour batter into bread pan and cover with foil. Place the pan in the slow-cooker. Pour water around the bread pan, about ¼ of the way up the sides of pan. Cook on HIGH for 3 to 4 hours, until bread is firm and toothpick inserted comes out clean. Remove and let cool, then take the bread out of pan, slice, and serve.

From Nicole's mother-in-law's kitchen

Homemade Applesauce

Once you taste Shannon's slow-cooked applesauce, you'll never buy the jarred version again.

Ingredients

8 to 10 large apples, peeled and cut into chunks

1 cup sugar

½ cup water

1 teaspoon cinnamon

Directions

Combine apples, sugar, water, and cinnamon in the slow-cooker. Stir gently. Cover and cook on LOW for 6 to 8 hours, or until apples are tender. Mash to desired consistency.

Submitted by Shannon Haines

Tapioca Pudding

When it's done cookin', ladle this tummy-yummy pudding into serving-size bowls and chill in the fridge (if you can wait, that is!).

Ingredients

2 quarts 1% milk (half-gallon)

1½ cups white sugar

1 cup small pearl tapioca

3 eggs

1 teaspoon vanilla

Directions

In a 4-quart or larger-size slow-cooker, combine the milk, sugar, and tapioca pearls. Stir well to mix. Cover and cook on HIGH for 2 to 5 hours, or until tapioca are soft. (The mixture will not be very thick.) In a separate bowl, mix the eggs with the vanilla. Take ½ cup of the hot milk and tapioca mixture and whisk it into the egg bowl. Repeat that same process two more times. Pour the contents of the egg-bowl into the slow-cooker; whisk until it is all thoroughly combined. Cover the slow-cooker and cook on HIGH for another 30 to 45 minutes, or until the tapioca is pudding-like in consistency. Unplug the slow-cooker and let sit for about an hour to cool.

Submitted by Dawn Bockelman

Fresh Fruit Cobbler

You'll fall in love with Maggie's reinvented version of this old-fashioned dessert.

Ingredients

1 stick butter, melted

1 cup self-rising flour

1 cup sugar

1 cup milk

fresh fruit (preferably peaches and/or blueberries, and/or blackberries)

nutmeg

Directions

Spray sides of the slow-cooker with a bit of non-stick cooking spray. Pour melted butter in the bottom of the slow-cooker. Pre-mix the flour, sugar, and milk, then pour over the butter. Cut up fresh fruit and cover the batter. Sprinkle with nutmeg. Cover and cook on HIGH for 3 to 4 hours.

Submitted by Maggie Irby Freshman

Triple Chocolate Mess

Ingredients

1 package chocolate cake mix

1 pint sour cream

1 package instant chocolate pudding

1 (6-ounce) bag chocolate chips

¾ cups oil

4 eggs

1 cup water

Directions

Spray the slow-cooker with non-stick cooking spray. Mix all the ingredients until smooth and pour into the slow-cooker. Cook on LOW for 6 to 8 hours. Remove the cooker from the base and let cool for 30 minutes or more (if you can resist!).

Submitted by Lia Odell

Black and Blue Cobbler

This berry-tastic dish is a cinch to throw together when comfort is what you crave.

Ingredients

1 cup all-purpose flour

1½ cups sugar, divided

1 teaspoon baking powder

¼ teaspoon salt

¼ teaspoon ground cinnamon

¼ teaspoon nutmeg

2 eggs, beaten

2 tablespoons milk

2 tablespoons vegetable oil

2 cups fresh or frozen blackberries

2 cups fresh or frozen blueberries

¾ cup water

1 teaspoon grated orange peel

Directions

In a bowl, combine flour, ¾ cup sugar, baking powder, salt, cinnamon, and nutmeg. In a separate bowl, combine eggs, milk, and oil; stir into dry ingredients just until moistened. Spread batter evenly onto the bottom of a greased 5-quart slow-cooker. In a saucepan, combine berries, water, orange peel, and remaining sugar; bring to a boil. Remove from the heat and immediately pour over the batter. Cover and cook on HIGH for 2 to 2½ hours, or until a toothpick inserted into the batter comes out clean. Turn off slow-cooker. Uncover and let stand for 30 minutes before serving. Makes 6 servings.

Submitted by Marcia Fischer

Hot Fudge Cake

When you're craving a yummo dessert that's as easy as it is delicious, this one hits the sweet spot.

Ingredients

1 cup packed brown sugar

1 cup flour

3 tablespoons cocoa powder

2 teaspoons baking powder

½ teaspoon salt

½ cup milk

2 tablespoons melted butter

½ teaspoon vanilla

Topping

¾ cup packed brown sugar

¼ cup unsweetened cocoa powder

1¾ cups boiling water

Directions

Mix together brown sugar, flour, cocoa powder, baking powder, and salt. Add milk, melted butter, and vanilla. Spread in the bottom of the slow-cooker. For topping, mix brown sugar and cocoa powder; sprinkle on top. Pour boiling water on top; do not stir. Cover and cook on HIGH for 2½ hours, or until a toothpick inserted in the center comes out clean. Serve warm with choice of topping. Can be doubled; if so, cook on HIGH for 3 hours.

Submitted by Lisa Willey

Apples 'n Port

Excellent hot or cold, this wine-infused dessert is a sublime ending to an elegant dinner.

Ingredients

4 to 6 whole cooking apples

½ cup raisins or currants

1 cup brown sugar

¼ teaspoon nutmeg

¼ teaspoon ground cinnamon

⅔ cup port wine

Directions

Core apples and cut a score around the sides about ⅓ of the way down from the top. Fill apple with raisins or currants and top with brown sugar, nutmeg, cinnamon, pressing the sugar lightly toward the center of the fruit. Place apples in the bottom of the slow-cooker and pour port over them, ensuring that some liquid goes into each apple center. Cover and cook on LOW for 3 to 4 hours, or until apples are soft. Pour excess port sauce over apples. Serve with vanilla ice cream or whipped cream.

Submitted by Steve & Margaret Crosby

Dump Cake

We were amazed at how effortless this is. Just throw in the ingredients and you're good to go!

Ingredients

1 can crushed pineapple, with juices

1 can cherry pie filling

1 box yellow cake mix

cinnamon

⅓ cup butter

Directions

Pour half the can of crushed pineapple, half the can of cherry pie filling, and half the box of cake mix into the slow-cooker; repeat the layers. Sprinkle with cinnamon and then dot with butter. Cover and cook on HIGH for 2 to 3 hours. Serve with ice cream and nuts, if preferred.

Submitted by Mishelle Shires

Index

CHICKEN

CHILI

CHOCOLATE

CORN

D

DESSERTS

DIPS

E

EGGS

Index

S

SANDWICHES

SAUCES

SAUSAGE

SIDES

SOUPS

STEWS

T

TOMATOES

TURKEY

V

VEGETABLES

Happy Crockin' Y'all!

One of the main reasons we started Crockin' Girls was to help families get back together around the dinner table. Life gets busy and trying to find the time to cook and enjoy meals together gets difficult. We hope these recipes allow you to spend less time in the kitchen and more time with the ones you love. Thanks for letting us into your homes!